CW00497912

WISDOM FOR LEADERSHIP
FAITH, VALUES AND HIGH PERFORMANCE

Tony Nelson
Moneer Hameed Tolephih

WISDOM FOR LEADERSHIP
FAITH, VALUES AND HIGH PERFORMANCE

Tony Nelson
Moneer Hameed Tolephih

CLARITAS
BOOKS

1 2 3 4 5 6 7 8 9 10

CLARITAS BOOKS

Bernard Street, Swansea, United Kingdom
Milpitas, California, United States

CLARITAS
BOOKS

© CLARITAS BOOKS 2021

This book is in copyright. Subject to statutory exception and to the provisions
of relevant collective licensing agreements, no reproduction of any part may
take place without the written permission of
Claritas Books.

First Published in January 2021

Typeset in Minion Pro 14/11

Wisdom for Leadership: Faith, Values and High Performance
By Tony Nelson & Moneer Hameed Tolephih

A CIP catalogue record for this book is available from the British Library

ISBN: 978-1-80011-991-8

Dedication

To my wife and soul-mate Kathy, for your
unfailing encouragement and support

Contents

The Holy Qur'an quotations unless otherwise stated are from *The Holy Qur'an : Translated by Abdullah Yusuf Ali, (2000),* Wordsworth Classics of World Literature.

Bible Scripture quotations marked (NIV) are taken from the Holy Bible, New International Version®, NIV®. Copyright © 1973, 1978, 1984, 2011 by Biblica, Inc.™ Used by permission of Zondervan. All rights reserved worldwide. www.zondervan.com The "NIV" and "New International Version" are trademarks registered in the United States Patent and Trademark Office by Biblica, Inc.™

Endorsements

'This book has successfully acknowledged the extricable relationship between faith and leadership practice and hence provides a truly enjoyable journey for leadership discovery and development. The book builds tangible and meaningful connections between values, faith and leadership theory. Indeed, it is a much welcomed perspective on how faith and values impact leadership practice and theory and it should be acknowledged that this has not had sufficient attention over the past few decades. This book brilliantly demonstrates how leadership cannot be separated from other aspects of humanity such as faith'

Ali Hadawi C.B.E.
Principal and Chief Executive
Central Bedfordshire College

'Wisdom for Leadership describes the story of the birth of the Deans Qualifying Programme (DQP) in Iraq and its roll out to a wider group of our senior leaders in Colleges and Schools. DQP helped transform the leadership capabilities of our people at a critical time in the country's development of its vocational education system. The benefits of this programme continue to this day. Tony poured his heart and soul into this vital work and that is reflected in his writing. I commend the book.'

H.E. Prof. Mahmood Al-Mullakhalaf,
Ambassador, Permanent Delegate of Iraq to
UNESCO in Paris and former President of
Foundation for Technical Education in Baghdad, Iraq

It was a great honour to participate in the Rawabit ('Partnership') Symposium in Istanbul in late 2011. Educators from the UK and Iraq had come together to talk a common language about the importance of education and how to improve the student experience at a time of great turmoil for Iraq. Tony and Moneer were present along with participants of the Deans Qualifying Programme. Wisdom for Leadership now brings their story of strengthening educational leadership in Iraq to a wider audience.

Education is a precious asset for any society. Kurds and Iraqis often talk about completing their education by which they mean obtaining a Doctorate. As an Honorary Professor at Soran University, I have seen their enthusiasm at first hand there and at other universities and schools.

I have visited Iraqi Kurdistan over 30 times since 2006, including parliamentary fact-finding missions in which we focused on education in schools and universities as well as at refugee and internally displaced people's camps. I know that very many people crave quality education. I well remember the young man I met in a rain-sodden and muddy park of temporary tents in Erbil. He had just fled from Mosul ahead of its takeover by Daesh. He explained in fluent English that he was just a couple of modules away from receiving his degree and wondered if he'd ever be able to do so.

After so many decades of dictatorship in Iraq and isolation in Kurdistan after they escaped Saddam Hussein in 1991, it is obvious that experience and expertise will take time to make a deeper difference to the quality of education. The work of Rawabit played an important role but there remains much to be done. Wisdom for Leadership documents how Iraqi educational leaders are making a unique contribution to help meet those challenges.

Gary Kent
Secretary, All-Party Parliamentary Group on Kurdistan
London
(writing in a personal capacity)

Acknowledgements

There are so many people who have accompanied me on this leadership development journey. Special thanks are due to:

- My Royal Mail teams in West London area, Watford St Albans and Enfield area, and also my UK Planning team
- The late David Legge who transformed my view of leadership by 'catching people doing things right'.
- Jacqui Henderson C.B.E. for giving me opportunity to experiment with leadership at the Learning and Skills Council (London Central) and also my wonderful team there who ran with the high performance concept, taking it to the next level
- The colleagues who worked with me on the Principals Qualifying Programme at the Centre for Excellence in Leadership which became LSIS (including Chief Executive Dr. Lynne Sedgmore, Janine Capaldi and Amy Gentles-McKie).
- My tutors on Strathclyde University's MBA (with a specialism in Leadership Studies) which helped me develop an academic underpinning for my high performance model - especially Prof. Roger Gill and (now) Prof. Gareth Edwards
- The Leadership Trust Foundation for immersing me in experiential learning as part of the MBA and the subsequent privilege of becoming a LTF tutor
- Dr Mahmood, whose vision for the Iraqi Deans Qualifying Programme provided the 'igniting spark' for the

programme and whose ongoing sponsorship affirmed its high priority within the Foundation for Technical Education. You are a father to DQP.

- Professor Moneer who as group leader for DQP, and later as Chief Assessor, provided guidance and wisdom to facilitators and delegates alike. You hosted us in Iraq and ensured our personal safety and welfare. It has been a privilege, dear brother, to work with you on this book.
- For Iraqi policy makers Dr. Kawther; Mr Saad Ibrahim; Mr Ahmed Gal; Mr Yousif; Dr. Abdul Kadhum and Dr. Rostom for your unfailing support for the DQP and HQP programmes and its wider rollout in Iraq.
- Dr. Nageb T. Rassam for your hand of Christian kindness and fellowship
- Jo Clough – who through endless coordination and influencing ensured that Rawabit always had a 'home' and sponsorship. You were a bridge between complex worlds and a source of encouragement in times of difficulty.
- Ali Hadawi C.B.E. – who by sharing his PQP experience with Iraqi colleagues through 'Rawabit' sowed the seeds which grew into the Iraqi DQP.
- Geoff Pine, Rawabit Chair, for enabling DQP to launch as a priority Rawabit programme
- Gary Kent, Secretary of the UK's All Party Parliamentary Group (APPG) on Kurdistan, for your interest in the programme and its development
- Martin Doel & John Mountford at the Association of Colleges, who adopted Rawabit and DQP into the AoC family
- The many UK Principals who so generously provided a week of leadership shadowing in UK Colleges for Iraqi Deans and Heads
- Chartered Manager Assessors Gaynor Thomas and John Sephton of the Chartered Management Institute (CMI) who coped with uncertainties as well as assessing in the

unfamiliar circumstances of Istanbul. Your empathy and warmth was exceptional. CMI support for the programme was outstanding.

- DQP assessors for the pilot phase of the programme, Howard Petch and the late Reg Chapman. Your insights, challenges and developmental feedback have been a gift to the programme and the Deans. I deeply valued your wisdom.
- Dave Peel and John Ashford (tutors in Iraq) and Larry Shulman(UK only) - for their hard work, support and contribution
- Peter Derbyshire for his 'scene-setting' work with me during the Iraqi FTE policy makers' exploratory visit in 2009
- Many colleagues at The British Council in Iraq for your logistical support which made delivery so much easier – you know who you are
- UK government's Department for Business Innovation and Skills, UNESCO, British Council and EU as main funders of phases of the programme
- The nine members of the pilot programme, who went on to become coaches and assessors to support the roll out of DQP and HQP. I am in awe at your humility, courage, professionalism and willingness to learn along with the ways you shared your wisdom. I treasure your warm friendship. You have a very special place in my heart and prayers.

- Dr. Moneer Hameed Tolephih
- Dr. Mohammad Nasser Ismael Nasser
- Dr. AbdulMuhssan Naji Al-ajeeli
- Dr. Fadhil Abdul Abbass Abidy
- Dr. Aziz Abed Abbas
- Dr. Fekri Najeeb Younis Al-Taweel
- Dr. Mohammed Fakhri Sa'ad Aldeen
- Dr. Rifat Mohammed Dakhil
- Dr. Kareem Ibrahim Al-kumai

- And of course to the amazing and talented Iraqi Deans and Head Teachers on DQP and HQP who were willing to move from simply 'being taught' to taking responsibility for your own leadership learning and development. You are shining examples for your colleagues and nation.
- Thanks to Mr Sherzad and Mr Hewa for your hospitality in Erbil
- Special thanks to my very dear friends Dr. Fadhil Ahmed Mohialdeen, Dr Affan Othman Hussein and Prof. Mudhaffar Sadiq Hassan. You have become brothers to me.
- To Prof. John Adair whose writing on leadership has influenced me throughout my working life. It was John who pointed me to Claritas Books.
- The team at Claritas Books, especially Wali-Ur Rahman, for sharing my vision for the manuscript.
- Several people have given me constructive feedback on the drafts. I am deeply grateful for their sharp eyes and insightful comments but any mistakes which remain in the text are of course mine.

Tony Nelson CMgr FCMI FRSA MBA/LS is an international leadership development consultant. Tony was programme director for the Deans and Heads Qualifying Programmes in Iraq, Istanbul and the UK between 2009 and 2013 – an intensive leadership development initiative for senior leaders of Iraqi Technical Universities, Colleges and Schools working in partnership with British Council, UNESCO, EU, Association of Colleges, Chartered Management Institute and Rawabit (a UK group supporting the advancement of excellence in Iraq's vocational education sector). As Director of the Principals Qualifying Programme in England he led a team supporting the executive leadership development of over 150 Principals and Chief Executives from the UK's learning and skills sector. He has extensive experience of leading and supporting change. He headed a consultancy specialising in high performance leadership. He was Director of Skills and Workforce Development for the Learning & Skills Council in central London and held senior roles in Royal Mail. He holds a MBA with a specialism in Leadership Studies from Strathclyde University. He holds a Diploma in Performance Coaching (Business) and Henley Business School's Management Diploma. He has tutored on a MSc in 21st Century Leadership. He is a Chartered Manager, Fellow of the Chartered Management Institute and a Fellow of the Royal Society of Arts.

Tony lives with his wife Kathy in Dorset and has five adult sons and five grandchildren.

Professor Moneer Hameed Tolephih Ph.D CMgr FCMI is President of the University of Baghdad – the largest higher education institution in the country. Previous leadership roles have included President of Al-Ayen University, President of Kerbala University and Dean of the Technical College, Baghdad.

Prof. Moneer was a key member of the policy maker group which visited the UK in 2009 to investigate the possibility of commissioning a customised version of the PQP programme for Iraq. Prof. Moneer was the senior Iraqi coach on the DQP programme. He was also Chief Assessor of written assignments submitted in the roll out of the DQP and HQP programmes. Prof. Moneer taught on these programmes which included a workshop he wrote focused on the leadership of the Prophet Muhammad (pbuh) which has now informed a chapter in this book.

Foreword

It has been my pleasure to know Tony and his work for some years now and when he invited me to write this forward I was truly honoured, as I know how his work has had the most important impact over the years. This impact is fundamentally important in how leadership studies, development and learning finds itself in the current time. For a while now the development of leaders has started to turn more towards understanding context and culture and away from developing leaders devoid of their own situation. The work Tony has developed with Professor Moneer Hameed Tolephih has been at the forefront of this wave of change and I am so glad to see that they have written up their experiences in the excellent, informative and inspirational book. I know this work as I have invited Tony to guest lecture on the courses I have the pleasure of leading at the Bristol Business School where we are engaging students in a context rich, socially constructed interpretation of leadership. His lectures over the years have epitomised this and helped students understand that leadership is not just about single strong leaders but about the inter-relationship and interpretation of leader-follower relationships in context and bounded by culture and language. My students would continually feedback to me that they found Tony's lectures helped them see this inter-relationship and interpretative view of leadership and I believe this book will do the same for you as the reader, I hope you enjoy the experience.

A second aspect that is important about the work that Tony

and Moneer explore in this book is the outcome of crisis. They show how leadership as a socially constructed term is intertwined with moments of change and upheaval. That is not to say that leadership is dictated by crisis and change but the development and learning of those in positions of responsibility have been undoubtedly helped by the interventions provided over the years. This impact is a testament to the commitment of both Tony and his team and their focus on important aspects of learning such as reflection, coaching and the pursuit of trust and wisdom. The book has lessons too for those involved in change of this nature and will help you, the reader, to negotiate the pressure you will feel in that position of responsibility and provide the basis for you to lead in an appropriate and ethical way.

Lastly, and fundamental to the experience explored in this book, is the ultimate connection leadership has with community and culture. I have for nearly twenty years now studied leadership from a dispersed and networked perspective, where we all have a responsibility to lead in many different ways. I have come to the conclusion that leadership is ultimately linked to community and the cultures that run across and between these communities. Hence leadership, in my mind, is inextricably linked to individuality and character in a personal sense, to friendship and ethics in a relational sense and to symbolism, liminality and language in a social sense. This book, for me, takes us on a journey that explores all of these aspects of leadership and leadership learning to enable us all to appreciate our role in our own communities which will enable us to work towards a sustainable society.

Gareth Edwards, Professor of
Leadership and Community Studies,
Bristol Business School, the University of
the West of England (UWE), UK

CHAPTER 1

A call to prayer

In August, 2014, I was working in the garden when my wife called me urgently into the house to "come and see the news". I watched on the television as a reporter explained that the terror group Daesh (Islamic State) was sweeping towards Erbil in Iraqi Kurdistan from their newly acquired base in Mosul. The Iraqi army had been overwhelmed in Mosul and Daesh was using captured weapons and equipment to support their push east to take Iraqi Kurdistan. I had worked in the Iraqi Kurdistan region since 2009 and knew so many people whose lives were now under imminent threat. I had been in the homes of Kurdish friends in Erbil and Sulaymaniyah. They had shared their family life with me. I had so many who counted me as a brother and yet on the screen I was watching the potential destruction of their communities. My Muslim, Christian, Arab, Kurdish and Turkmen friends were having their lives turned upside down. The Kurdistan region's Peshmerga ('those who face death') were the only effective fighting force that stood in the way of Daesh but they were under-manned and under-equipped against such a powerful and terrifying enemy. I prayed for God to intervene. Many others across the world were praying too, I am sure. I knew my Iraqi extended family members would also be offering prayers to God. Daesh were about 40 kilometres from Erbil.

For me this felt like the unfolding of a personal tragedy and I was powerless to help. But God was not powerless and He answered prayer. The American led coalition intervened with aerial bombardments which halted the Daesh advance and allowed the Peshmerga space to consolidate and build defensive positions. In time, additional supplies and ammunition reached the Peshmerga and then coalition forces began to support training of additional troops. The invasion into Iraqi Kurdistan had been halted and that showed Daesh could be resisted. The main Iraqi forces in the south regrouped and mobilised against the parallel threat to Baghdad and, with support from other countries, Daesh advances were similarly halted. It was of course not until October 2016 that Daesh in Mosul was defeated and the city liberated, with heavy fighting and many military and civilian casualties. I finally found out that the Mosul based college leader I knew had survived the conflict. I had been working in country since 2009 and Iraq and its people had won my heart. I was fascinated with Iraq's history and culture.

I had the privilege of bringing leadership development programmes to groups of senior educational leaders (Deans) from across Iraq and I had learned as much from my new brothers and sisters as they were learning from me. *Wisdom for Leadership* tells the story of this leadership development work in its unique and troubled setting. It recounts some of the human narratives and draws out the leadership wisdom acquired on that 'journey'. But it also has a wider purpose. *Wisdom for Leadership* is written for managers across the Middle East and beyond who want to reflect on and strengthen their personal practice of leadership. Much of the world's leadership literature has a Western European or North American focus because that is where the majority of leadership research, development and commentary has taken place but inevitably those insights developed have a particular world view. David Weir writes 'It is time for Western scholarship to look more broadly and with greater understanding at the bases of culture and belief systems that exist inside as well as outside its traditional home. The need to re-engage with other cultures of leadership is urgent' (Weir in Turnbull et al, 2012). *Wisdom for*

Leadership takes some of the best and most relevant leadership learning from around the world, including that of Middle East and non-Western scholars, and places it clearly and accessibly in a faith-based context. It is based on the experience of designing and delivering leadership development programmes in Iraq and elsewhere. Whilst delivering programmes in the Middle East I discovered it was impossible to separate 'leadership' from other essential aspects of living. I found in the Middle East that there was just life with no secular lens. Life to Islamic leaders and managers for example embraced faith, family, science, work, management, leadership, health and so much more. In the Middle East leadership is truly integrative. In the Western world leadership development more typically takes a secular approach to executive learning. The leadership development conversations I experienced with Islamic managers over several years were powerfully enriched by a mutual sharing of faith. I was introduced to the concept of the 'people of the Book' and began to understand that Islamic, Christian and Jewish traditions and beliefs have more in common than in difference. They share Abrahamic roots which are ancient and deep. We have much to learn from one another. Metcalfe and Murfin (in Metcalfe and Mimouni, 2011) write 'within Islamic states…faith, devotion and the sacred are integral to the practice of leadership and to revealing the qualities of that leadership'. Their book *Leadership Development in the Middle East* was the first text published in English on the subject of leadership development in the Middle East (drawing on both English and Arabic scholarship) and it has helped shape my reflections on the leadership programmes I directed.

The Middle East is intensely relational and I found it was important to build trust early on and invest time in one to one relationships with key opinion formers. Leadership learning without these enablers in place would only be superficial. Transformative leadership learning took place when delegates felt safe, respected and understood. This book therefore has strong spiritual anchors which respect Islamic tradition and wisdom about leadership. At the core of the book is the intensely human story of a leadership development programme I had the privilege of designing and delivering in Iraq.

This Iraq programme received international coverage and featured in a major article in the UK's prestigious newspaper *The Sunday Times* (Chynoweth, 2011) and was also a finalist in the USA's Management Mix competition for innovation in management in 2012. The story of the pilot programme was recounted in an article I wrote for the international management journal *Developing Leaders* (Nelson & Peel, 2011b)

'The challenge was to deliver a culturally sensitive, relevant and challenging program which would help Iraqi Deans develop the leadership skills they needed to build high performance teams, lead change, engage with key external stakeholders including employers, grow income…..and become reflective leadership practitioners. And all this in an environment of 'post-liberation reconstruction' (their description) in which Deans warranted bodyguards as representatives of the government. The Deans had stories of assassination attempts against them, repeatedly looted Colleges, students taken hostage, and subsequent negotiations with insurgent leaders to de-politicise the campus. These stories would come to us over morning tea ('chai') or during an evening walk. This was their life and they were sharing it with us.

The Deans said that what they most wanted was hope as they had suffered decades of dictatorship and then imposed democracy – all of which had failed to live up to their expectations. I felt humbled by their experience under such adversity, but honoured to be trusted to help them seek new inspiration. These leaders were impacting a generation of young people and former insurgents and their leadership would help rebuild this hurting nation. I began to develop a sense of the strategic impact this leadership program could have at such a critical point in the country's history.

In an Iraqi group the key to meaningful learning is to establish trusting, respectful relationships. It was as if (we) had been invited into an extended family. Nevertheless, we still had to establish personal and professional credibility, developing our own bonds based around a profound respect for Iraqi culture and showing that we would learn alongside the Deans. Building those relationships was a layered process – for example, we noticed stronger attachments on each occasion we visited Iraq. We were placing our safety in the hands of our hosts and affording them a chance to show traditional hospitality.

The role of a group leader in Iraqi culture is very different to the UK. A group leader has palpable authority 'for the journey', a concept emanating from the Qur'an. It is essential to understand and acknowledge this, consulting the group leader for all important decisions and briefing them ahead of modules, changes and key activities. Faith is part of the Iraqi culture (mainly Sunni and Shia Muslim with some Christian communities) though some Deans are more overt in their faith than others. We were working with people from the land of the Tower of Babel, city of Nineveh (Mosul) and great biblical figures such as Noah, Abraham, Daniel and Esther. It was from here three wise men travelled to find a baby Jesus. I determined to honour that past, reconnecting Deans with their own leadership heritage, whilst introducing new thinking. We found spirituality to be an inseparable part of Iraqi leadership wisdom. The five calls to prayer each day were an audible reminder of this. The Deans were deeply moved to receive in Arabic a personal copy of (John Adair's) book the 'The Leadership of Muhammad'.

This is an extract from an article originally published in *Developing Leaders* Quarterly in 2011 available at www.developingleadersquarterly.com and is used with permission.

I was humbled to listen to their personal stories of saying good-bye to their families each morning, never knowing if this was to be their last day on this earth. They were seeking to make a difference in the lives of students, de-politicise their campuses, resolve tribal disputes, manage student accommodation, achieve high educational outcomes...... and survive one day at a time. 'In-sha'Allah' (God's will) was never far from their lips. I was drawn to these dignified, gentle, faithful professionals who simply wanted to learn about leadership.

'Regret looks back. Fear looks around. Worry looks in. Faith looks up'

(Nicky Gumbel)

I found the Iraqi Deans to be people who 'looked up' in faith.

In order to be a source of useful learning for Deans every aspect of their leadership programme needed to be contextualised for a Middle East, Islamic, mainly Arab group. This contextualisation took place beforehand when possible but in the pilot it often occurred as a 'work in progress' in the classroom. As tutors we quickly realised we were on as steep a learning curve as our Iraqi colleagues. Iraq had been isolated from the outside world for decades and during the programme we discovered that Deans had been raised on didactic teaching methods so our informal style of learner-centred delivery was ground-breaking for them.

It is my hope that this book will stimulate readers in the Middle East and elsewhere to seek their own answers to the question of 'what is wisdom for leadership?'. I hope the reader will pause to reflect on their own leadership practice. It is a huge challenge to lead any organisation or team in the complexity of today's Middle East settings. The wisest leaders reflect on their practice so that they can constantly improve.

Wisdom for Leadership has a primary focus on organisational leadership. I have therefore avoided much direct comment on issues of leadership outside organisations unless it is contextually needed. There are other writers who are better qualified than I to write about political leadership. However, my belief is that strengthening the capability and capacity of leaders of organisations in the public service and business will have an impact on wider leadership by showing what is possible and stimulating demand for something better from political leaders. *Wisdom for Leadership* seeks to help the busy leader articulate meaning and purpose in the workplace. It is written with diagnostics and practical leadership tools for the reader to use in his or her team or organisation.

Napoleon Bonaparte said:

'The only way to lead is to show people the future. A leader is a dealer in hope'.

If this book helps leaders increase hope in their workplaces across the Middle East and beyond it will have achieved its purpose.

Tony Nelson
Dorset, October 2020

CHAPTER 2

Why do we need Leadership?

'The importance of good leadership today hardly needs to be stressed. For it is widely recognised that a democratic society cannot work effectively without it. Leaders are needed in all fields and at all levels to give direction, create teamwork and inspire people to give of their best'

(Adair, 1989)

Organisations need leaders. Great organisations need great leadership. The bigger an organisation, the more it needs effective leadership at every level. Board members and chief executives will exercise leadership by developing ambitious strategic plans; departmental and team leaders will exercise leadership by helping their groups deploy those plans. When effective leadership is practised at every level of an organisation it becomes balanced.

'Soldiers without a leader are like sheep without a shepherd'

(Sumerian clay tablet)

This ancient leadership parable is taken from the earliest known writing in the world, which is over 5000 years old. It is the first recorded 'wisdom' about leadership and it comes from Babylon, Iraq.

There are many definitions of leadership but the modern one

I like the most has been developed at the UK's Leadership Trust who say that leadership is:

'Using our personal power to win the hearts and minds of those around us to achieve a common purpose'.

It has been said that 'you can be appointed a commander or a manager but you are not a leader until your appointment has been ratified in the hearts and minds of those you lead' (Adair, 2010). The job of a leader is to help people align their effort with the shared aims of the organisation which employs them. To do that the leader needs to explain how people's work contributes towards the organisation's purpose. A leader connects people with purpose. Al-Azami (2019) writes of the prophet Muhammad: 'He won hearts not arguments'. Such leadership is too scarce today.

Are leaders born or made? The 'nature versus nurture' argument has been debated for years but what is certain is that every leader has indeed been born! I think the answer to the question lies somewhere in the middle with the most effective leaders having some innate talent for leadership which has then been developed through training and reflective practice. The best orchestral musicians are those who have a passion for music, a good ear and have then applied themselves to learning and practice over many years. Leadership is similar – strong natural aptitude is a good place to start but is not enough on its own. It has to be developed, practiced and reflected on. A proverb of the Bambileke people in West Africa (in Adair, 2020) says:

'You are not born a leader, you become one'

Many copy what they admire in those leaders for whom they have worked or consciously avoid replicating damaging practice from leaders whose approach they did not like. However, few take time to reflect in a structured way. Leadership development programmes give a space for leaders to do that, ideally alongside other leaders. Adair (2018) observes 'it takes a long time to become a born leader!' The Qur'an recognises leadership when God says 'And we raise some above others in rank so that some may command work from others' (43:32).

The most pressing challenge today is for organisations to develop leadership skills. Modern leadership development relies less on taught modules and programmes and much more on helping leaders acquire the skills to make sense of a rapidly changing world. This includes peer training, reflective enquiry and coaching. Leaders become learners, who learn most from other leaders. These leaders take responsibility for their professional leadership development. Organisations have in the past relied on bureaucracy, compliance with instructions, clear lines of authority and hierarchy to get things done. This worked well in a stable environment in which little changed and everyone understood the boundaries for action. But life has moved on and we live today in a rapidly changing age of global markets, high-speed internet communications, mobile 'apps', economic and political instabilities and instant consumer feedback on social media. Technology is removing market barriers to entry so that organisations are facing competition from new entrants able to charge lower prices and offer superior service. The Covid-19 global pandemic has put leaders under intense pressure as governments, organisations, teams and individuals seek to adapt to survive. Some leaders have risen to these challenges and yet others have crumbled. It has been observed that character is not formed in a crisis but rather it is revealed by it. The same could be said of leadership. We need to continually invest in leadership (including our focus on values and what we call 'character') so that we can weather the storms which lie ahead.

Organisations need leadership to be agile and adaptive to challenges. These leaders need to influence effectively to increase collaboration and commitment within their teams. Entrepreneurs are said to influence beyond the resources they have; in the same way leaders exercise influence beyond what they directly manage. They are the true influencers of today. Such agile leadership can only operate successfully in a high-trust, supportive environment.

'If your actions inspire others to dream more, learn more, do more and become more, you are a leader'

(John Quincy Adams)

❧ The Changing Role Of Leadership And Cultures In The Middle East

Today's executives need to rely less on command and control approaches in order to better engage an increasingly educated and informed workforce who do not want to be 'told' what to do or believe. Globalisation of study and work is encouraging people to challenge accepted forms of authority. The internet is providing access to new knowledge. This means that positional power (hierarchical authority) is becoming less important. Whilst specific cultural norms vary from country to country, old styles of leadership are not as effective as they once were.

Across the Middle East new voices are being heard, demanding change. The Arabic-speaking world has some of the world's highest rates of youth unemployment. In the West, leadership is slowly changing to meet the demands of struggling economies, emerging technologies and many disengaged employees. In Brazil, Russia, India and China leaders grapple with the opposite challenges of high-growth and the social dislocation this brings as their economies rapidly urbanise. Work is changing. Social structures are breaking down as vast numbers of peoples are displaced, or migrate, seeking security or a better life. Leadership has to be able to re-invent itself to meet the needs of the people it serves. My hope is that this book will help you strengthen your leadership skills to better adapt in your own setting – whether that is leading a team or an organisation in the Middle East of elsewhere.

'Your position never gives you the right to command. It only imposes on you the duty of so living your life that others can receive your orders without being humiliated'

(Dag Hammarskjold, former UN Secretary-General, 1964)

Young people entering the labour market today are bringing a capacity for digital communication and electronic networking which is unprecedented. However, their inter-personal skills in a face to face or team setting may not be as advanced so leaders must find effective ways to communicate with this generation. 'Telling' such people what to do is unlikely to succeed. The new leadership skills call for work to be explained; tasks to have meaning; people to be given development opportunities. The Middle Eastern skills of story-telling and building trusting relationships will be of great value in this emerging leadership model.

The public sector has multiple stakeholders who need to be engaged in meaningful partnerships, making personal influencing a key leadership skill rather than relying on formal positional power. This collaborative environment can be tough as it requires huge amounts of emotional investment and energy. There is however a deep tradition of consultative leadership within much Middle Eastern heritage which gives a solid foundation to tackle these new problems.

'Forgive them, and pray for them, and take consult from them in all matters of public concern'

(Qur'an 3:159)

This book will give you an opportunity to reflect on your effective use of leadership power and the appropriate balance between positional and personal power for you as you serve those you lead.

'The servant-leader is servant first...It begins with the natural feeling that one wants to serve, to serve first....The best test is: Do those served grow as persons? Do they, while being served, become healthier, wiser, freer, more autonomous, more likely themselves to become servants? And what is the effect on the least privileged in society; will they benefit?

(Greenleaf, 1970)

Leadership in Islam is a trust - 'amanah' - which embraces the idea of trust and responsibility towards stakeholders. Adair (2010) argues for truth and integrity as a fundamental to create trust in leadership. Individuals should speak the truth, keep one's promise, fulfil one's trust, practice modesty and behave justly (see Qur'an 12:54-55) write Metcalfe and Murfin (in Metcalfe and Mimouni, 2011) and Islamic leaders have 'two primary functions; as servant leaders and as guardian leaders'.

'truly the best of men for thee to employ is the (man) who is strong (competent) and trusty'

(Qur'an, 88:26)

How we personally exercise power as a leader is crucial in setting the culture and tone of an organisation or team. We will explore this issue later and look at leadership wisdom in the life of the Prophet, peace be upon him (pbuh). There is increasing discussion in Western academic and leadership studies circles of the importance of non-Western forms of leadership in an attempt to rediscover the leadership wisdoms of more ancient civilisations.

This book seeks to draw from this body of wisdom.

High impact leaders draw on a range of styles appropriate to the circumstances. This flexibility is part of being an adaptive leader. The high performance literature points to styles which are attuned to emotional intelligence in individuals and teams i.e. visionary, democratic, coaching and affiliative leadership styles. There is a move away from the leader being seen as 'the expert' (which only creates dependency). This book introduces models of leadership which will help readers maximise their impact in the longer term - these are relational and social models of leadership. This is in tune with Arab and Islamic tradition and seeks to avoid the 'dominant Western conceptualizations of leadership and management' (Metcalfe and Mimouni, 2011) who write:

> *'the administrative system in most Arab countries suffers from underdeveloped governance practices characterised by a lack of transparency in decision making, absence of professional human resources and leadership development systems and an overall lack of systematic management processes and procedures. However, when solutions are brought in to 'fix' this situation, they are usually imported from the West and incorporate a different set of underlying values and assumptions about human behaviour, motivation and leadership dynamics, and have little knowledge of the cultural nuances peculiar to the region. Hence the pivotal importance of a culturally appropriate model of leadership development in most Middle East countries'*

> *(Metcalfe and Mimouni, 2011)*

They argue that the 'Middle East leader must be, to some extent a bricoleur; he must work with what is to hand because the tools which may be procured from the West for the development of leadership contain certain embedded assumptions which are not necessarily relevant'. Wiktionary defines a bricoleur as 'one who creates using whatever materials are available'. Informal Networks (2009) write: 'In France, bricoleurs sit somewhere between a handy man and a jobbing builder. Whereas an architect normally begins with a clean sheet of paper, and designs from scratch to meet a specified requirement, the bricoleur always begins with an existing building, in whatever state it is, and makes it better.' I saw many of the Iraqi Deans and Head Teachers acting as a bricoleur during leadership workshops, in their written assignments, action learning projects and in their assessment evidence for Chartered Manager status.

Effectiveness as a leader involves empowering other people within a framework. The framework developed by the early successors to the Prophet (Ali in Metcalfe and Mimouni, 2011) saw leadership responsibility as a civic duty, with leadership as a shared influence, a reciprocal relationship and an attribution phenomenon in which people 'attribute' particular qualities to those they follow. These early ideas about leadership in an Islamic setting form a very powerful image for the modern practitioner to reflect on. 'Societies differ in their perception of leadership and what makes an effective leader. Hofstede (1999) for example, notes that such differences are primarily determined by cultural values.' (Ali in Metcalfe and Mimouni, 2011). Arab culture has in many studies been described as high in 'power-distance' (Hofstede, 1980, 1991) and in such cultures there is typically an emphasis on bureaucratic systems with an unnecessary numbers of organisational layers. Arab culture places great reliance on individual relationships, the public saving of face, with greater priority given to family, the group and community than that afforded to the individual (Metcalfe and Minoumi, 2011). Reliance in the Middle East on the public sector to provide employment for most people means that private sector dynamics for efficiency, responsiveness and adaptability are often weak.

'A ruler who has been entrusted with the affairs of Muslims,
but makes no endeavour for their material and moral uplift

and is not concerned for their welfare will not enter paradise with them'

(reported by Abu Malih in Sahih Muslim 1:82, Chapter 44, Hadith no 264)

Beekun and Badawi's (1999) work on leadership in an Islamic context focused heavily on ethical and moral dimensions. Metcalfe and Minoumi (2011) list five core values which the Islamic leader should focus on; *'Birr* (fair dealing), *Amanah* (trust), *'Adl* (justice), *Mujahadah* (self-improvement) and *'Ahd* (integrity and keeping one's word)'. This is reinforced by Abuznaid and Weir (in Metcalfe and Mimouni, 2011) who studied leadership in a Jordanian context. They write 'a key feature of an effective leader in an Islamic context is one who displays humility and compassion and who values consensus-oriented decision making. However, the leader is the guardian, one who presides over the spiritual, moral and intellectual development of his community'.

Martin Luther King Jr said this about the importance of service:

'If you want to be important—wonderful. If you want to be recognized—wonderful. If you want to be great—wonderful. But recognize that he who is greatest among you shall be your servant. That's a new definition of greatness. By giving that definition of greatness, it means that everybody can be great, because everybody can serve. You don't have to have a college degree to serve. You don't have to make your subject and your verb agree to serve. You don't have to know about Plato and Aristotle to serve. You don't have to know Einstein's theory of relativity to serve. You don't have to know the second theory of thermodynamics in physics to serve. You only need a heart full of grace, a soul generated by love. And you can be that servant.'

(speech delivered at Atlanta, Georgia on 4 February 1968)

Leaders everywhere can learn from these words of wisdom.

❧ Leadership Reflection

'Those who cannot remember the past are condemned to repeat it'.

(Santayana, 1905)

How do you connect with your own personal leadership history?

On a piece of paper, represent your leadership learning journey and feelings about leadership over the last few years using a timeline like this one. Plot two or three key events affecting your leadership of people and what you felt about those experiences.

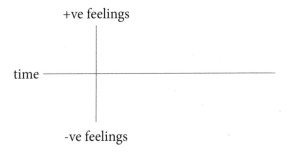

As you reflect on these events what is the key learning for you as a leader? What do you choose to avoid in future and what do you choose to build into your own leadership practice?

One of the best ways to increase your personal store of leadership wisdom is to reflect on your leadership practice. Reflective practice is used in many professions to draw out learning and to improve the delivery of services. It is a tool of immense value to leadership practitioners. Reflection is 'a form of mental processing or thinking....to fulfil a purpose' (Moon, 2006) who continues, 'reflection is applied to relatively complex or ill-structured ideas for which there is not an obvious solution'.

'Truth is the daughter of search'

(Arab Proverb)

Leadership reflection invites the leader to process their thoughts and feelings about people, events or challenges in order to learn from them and apply that developed wisdom in their future practice. There is often not a single correct answer but only a set of choices or options to consider. Leadership reflection considers the impact of our past choices on those we lead in order to make corrections to future choices. Corrections may be small or large. The point is that they are *our* corrections rather than imposed by outside forces. Metcalfe and Murfin (in Metcalfe and Mimouni, 2011) point to the Islamic tradition of feedback being thought of as a gift. It can be very helpful as we reflect to have the help of a trusted colleague or peer with whom personal leadership reflection is shared in confidence. You may want to keep a leadership learning journal in which you write down your key personal leadership lessons and insights. This journal will allow you to record your insights, thoughts and feelings as you read the book. What are you learning? What are the dynamics between your team members and how are you responding to that as a leader? What is your personal impact? If you keep a written journal it will be easier to develop your own leadership wisdom. You should keep it confidential and not identify named individuals.

Reflection then is your process of thinking about your leadership; *leadership learning* is the outcome of that reflection which in turn affects your *leadership practice*. It can be hard work to reflect, especially if your natural inclination is to take action rather than stop and think about things. Reflection may not feel like action and, if that is so, you may need to consciously give yourself permission to reflect.

'The ability to reflect and self-evaluate is to provide oneself with feedback'

(Eraut, 1994)

Beekun and Badawi (2009) emphasise the value of obtaining feedback and acting upon it, positioning this as part of the task of self-understanding for a Muslim, which they define as 'the ability to recognize one's strengths and compensate for one's weaknesses'. The Caliph Abu Bakr stated 'O people! I have been selected as your trustee although I am no better than any of you. If I am right, obey me. If I am misguided, set me right' (in Al Buraey, 1985). Goldsmith (2008) describes a series of flaws in leaders who once they are promoted to a senior role simply rely on the skills that got them there rather than in acquiring the new skills needed for their new role. One of these is 'an excessive need to be me (which is) exalting our faults as virtues simply because they're who we are'. In other words it is about rejecting honest feedback and turning it on its head by pretending that the flaw is a good thing. This is one of the worst forms of denial.

We can move ourselves from surface learning to deep learning through the process of reflection. Deep learning creates the possibility of leadership development and personal change. Deep learning is where personal leadership wisdom is discovered. Moon (2006) explains that surface learning is where we simply notice what is happening. As we move towards deeper learning we first need to make sense of what we are observing and then search for meaning in that. As we work with that meaning we begin the important process of transformative learning. Reflection therefore is not about simply adding new knowledge on top of old knowledge (like layers in a cake) but rather helping us make our learning personal and deeply integrated with our leadership practice. Reflection and learning are an essential component of leadership wisdom.

In the first empirical studies of the hard benefits of reflection on learning, Stefano & Gino et al (2014) found that reflection is a critical element of learning. Their studies conducted laboratory and field work experiments. Impact was measured in a mix of self-efficacy (perception), assessment tests during and after training and job performance. They describe reflection as an 'intentional attempt to synthesize, abstract and articulate key lessons taught by experience'. They found a performance differential greater than 20% when comparing learning by doing with learning by doing *with reflection*. Their study showed that reflecting on key lessons learned by experience boosts self-efficacy, which strengthens learning. These higher results were sustained over time. One of their key findings was that reflection made a significant difference in both performance and increased self-efficacy.

'There is more to life than simply increasing its speed'

(Ghandi)

❧ Leadership Learning

Leadership learning can be messy and is definitely non-linear. It is a mix of rational and emotional responses. We will explore gaps in how we perceive ourselves as a leader and how we are experienced by those who follow. Learning in this way can be uncomfortable. But it has been shown that it can be a very powerful means by which executives develop themselves. Effective leaders engage hearts and minds - both their own and that of others. Closing the gap between reality and perception is an important part of leadership learning.

'When God wishes a man well, he gives him insight into his faults'

(Arab Proverb)

Your leadership learning is not a quick fix or overnight transformation. Indeed to be effective it will demand effort and energy on your part along with good feedback from those you trust. Antanocopoulou and Bento (1994) place significance on what they call 'learning leadership, an approach to leadership that rests on transformational concepts, and where leadership is a process of becoming and learning is a way of being' (Metcalfe and Mimouni, 2011). Islamic ideals embrace 'the necessity of transforming capabilities, with the focus on humanistic development', write Metcalfe and Mimouni '... the implication is that, with respect to Islamic leadership, management training and development activities can provide the space for leadership learning to become emergent and to be discovered. It articulates the view that leadership development is a dynamic capability that can assist in social transformation of traditional leadership mindsets, and refocus Middle East leaders in public agencies and private organizations, not only to the task in hand, but to broader social and ethical agendas'. This is what Western (2008) calls a 'macro focus'.

Adair (2010) writes 'no-one is born wise; a leader becomes wise - acquires practical wisdom - through natural aptitude, practice and reflection'. Practical wisdom (*phronesis*) 'is essentially the practical judgement as to what to do and how to do it in a morally challenging situation' (Adair, 2018). As you follow the path laid out in this book you will find numerous opportunities to add to your store of wisdom drawn from research, case studies, and practice in Middle East and other Islamic settings. In his most recent book Adair (2020) explains that 'a practically wise person is always a doer, but one who acts with skill and judgment'. He writes that such practical wisdom 'enables us to discover what is good for the community at large'. Such a skillset is to be highly valued and resonates strongly with Islamic imperatives upon leaders to seek the wider good.

'Practical wisdom is an alchemist's mixture of intelligence, experience and goodness. It is the exercise of judgement on the highest level known to us'

(Adair, 2020)

My friend Bishop David, once said that learning 'is like eating fish - you spit out the bones and eat the flesh'. My reader's job is to work out what are the 'bones' in this book which can be ignored and what can be safely digested and absorbed. This metaphor reminds me of the delicious Masgouf fish I was introduced to which is a Mesopotamian river carp, typically cooked in a tandoor or over coals. It has the biggest fish bones I have ever seen. A single fish is shared between two people and eaten with the fingers. I once made the mistake of reaching over to the 'wrong' side to get some fish meat and was gently guided to the correct side! Eating in Iraq is a collaboration.

❧ Personal Leadership Development Plan

Reflection as a leader naturally moves us to seek personal development. Such momentum for personal change is a mark of maturity and part of the development of wisdom. Rumi is quoted in Al-Azami (2019) as saying:

'Yesterday I was clever, so I wanted to change the world. Today I am wise, so I am changing myself.'

You may wish to complete a personal leadership development plan to synthesise the learning you capture perhaps in your journal, using the diagnostics or from personal reflection in order to turn it into an actionable plan. Your plan is likely to be an iterative process as you engage with your learning. Some activities will be finished before others.

What will I do?	Who do I need to involve?	When will I start?	How will I know I have succeeded?	Progress

❧ Why do we need wisdom?

The online Cambridge Dictionary (2019) defines wisdom as *'the ability to use your knowledge and experience to make good decisions and judgements'*. The Key Differences (2019) website writes: 'Knowledge is the accumulation of information, learned through education or experience. On the other hand, wisdom is when you know how to apply your knowledge, for the benefit of others'. Banna writes in the prologue to Al-Azami (2019):

> 'Wisdom has no race, religion or geography, and is neither Western nor Eastern. Prophet Muhammad taught his followers that wisdom is actually the lost property of the believer and wherever it is found, it should be claimed and adopted'.

My hope is that this book will present the reader with wisdom drawn from many sources and that some of it will be 'claimed and adopted'. I will focus on three types of wisdom in this chapter: intrinsic, extrinsic and spiritual wisdom.

'Then shall every soul be paid what it earned, and none shall be dealt with unjustly'

(Qur'an, 2:281)

Intrinsic wisdom

This is inner wisdom we develop organically as we progress through life. It often increases with age. The prophet Job said:

'Wisdom is with the aged, and understanding in length of days'.

(Job 12:12, NIV)

Coaches working with a coachee will sometimes say that the 'answer lies within the coachee', which is a recognition of this inner wisdom. This type of wisdom is acquired and grown through experience. Many of our personal values and beliefs about leadership have been acquired by working for very good leaders (whose practices we try to copy) or very bad leaders (whose harmful practices we vow to avoid in our own leadership). These personal learnings are an example of acquired, intrinsic wisdom.

Extrinsic wisdom

This is the wisdom of others or of the outside world. It includes ancient wisdoms from tribes, elders, cultures and literature. Sometimes it has been handed down verbally and at other times it takes written form. The body of knowledge about leadership, for example, is a type of extrinsic wisdom upon which we can draw to help our work as leaders. This type of wisdom is handed down or acquired through study and research. Some of it will pass into our personal intrinsic wisdom 'store' as we process it and adopt it into our own leadership practice, values and beliefs. The leadership proverbs quoted in this book are examples of extrinsic wisdom.

Spiritual wisdom

This is wisdom whose source is from God. In Psalm 119: 97-98 (NIV) it says 'Oh how I love your law! It is my meditation all the day. Your commandment makes me wiser than my enemies, for it is ever with me'. The books of Psalms and Proverbs in the Bible are often referred to as 'Wisdom books' because they are full of spiritual wisdom. Many prophets were gifted with extraordinary spiritual wisdom including Moses, Daniel and Jesus. Their words contain powerful spiritual truths and insights which are still relevant today. The Prophet Solomon's wisdom was legendary and kings came from all over the known world to hear him. Friedman and Friedman (2019) write: 'A great leader is not concerned about building an empire through conquest but uses his wisdom to bring peace. A necessary prerequisite for peace is justice, and Solomon was universally known for his wisdom and justice'. When a leader gains spiritual wisdom it brings great blessings. The life of the prophet Joseph (Yusuf) illustrates this:

> 'Thus did We plan for Joseph. He could not take his brother by the law of the king except that Allah willed it (so). We raise to degrees (of wisdom) whom we please; but over all endued with knowledge is One, the All-Knowing'.

> (Qur'an 12:76)

Joseph suffered terribly over many years at the hands of his brothers and then from his Egyptian master. But God had a plan and in it all God was teaching Joseph lessons which would prepare him for a great position. Part of that plan was to give Joseph spiritual wisdom and insight which ultimately benefited nations. We can gain spiritual wisdom by studying and meditating on Holy Scripture; by participating in a community of faith with wise teachers; and in prayer and reflection.

The book of Proverbs says of wisdom:

'The fear of the LORD is the beginning of wisdom, and knowledge of the Holy One is understanding.'

(Proverbs 9:10, NIV)

In many countries and organisations today there is a need for wiser leadership. We need leaders who develop their stores of intrinsic, extrinsic and spiritual wisdom. Nelson Mandela is a powerful example of a leader who acquired all three types of wisdom in his life journey, much of it during his time in prison on Robben Island. He became a transformational leader of the first order, impacting the birth of a new South Africa as a 'rainbow nation'. The transfer of power from white minority rule to its black majority could have resulted in a bloodbath. Mandela's wise leadership was deeply grounded in tribal and spiritual wisdom, of which this is one of the most challenging examples:

'No one is born hating another person because of the colour of his skin, or his background, or his religion. People must learn to hate, and if they can learn to hate, they can be taught to love, for love comes more naturally to the human heart than its opposite'

(Nelson Mandela, 1995)

Mandela is stating truth which resonates as strongly today as when he spoke it. The Black Lives Matter movement is challenging societies globally to seek racial justice and equality. This will demand greater wisdom from leaders in every sphere of life.

Wisdom for Leadership brings together intrinsic, extrinsic and spiritual wisdoms using Eastern, Western and tribal voices. If we seek to develop and integrate all three of these wisdoms into our leadership practice it will help us serve better those we aspire to lead. There are tools in this book which can be used by leaders grappling with the challenge of leading teams and organisations through rapidly changing environments; the book shares wisdom for how to harness the talents, ideas and innovative capabilities of every team member. We are living in the most challenging period for organisational leaders, who need to build and maintain trust whilst adapting to new circumstances and ways of working.

❧ A word for younger leaders

Leadership responsibility at a young age or early part of your career is a great opportunity but it is also a challenge. Seeking formal training to accelerate your acquisition of wisdom is a sensible investment of your time and energy. Reading books like this one is another such investment and I hope that you will be encouraged to develop your reflective capacity through the services of a coach, mentor or other trusted colleague. Some people think that leadership is only learned through the experiences of life but that is a very slow method and it can be very costly to your career. Adair (2018) writes:

> 'Learning about leadership happens when sparks of relevance jump in between experience and practice on the one hand, and principles or theory on the other hand. One without the other tends to be sterile. It is a common fallacy that leadership is learnt only through experience. Experience only teaches the teachable, and it is a school which charges large fees. Sometimes people graduate from it when they are too old to apply the lessons. Leadership is far better learnt by experience and reflection or thought, which, in turn, informs or guides future

action. Other people, as examples or models, teachers or mentors, have an important part to play in this process.'

🕊 Key Wisdom in this chapter

- Great organisations and teams need great leaders
- Leadership is 'using our personal power to win the hearts and minds of those around us to achieve a common purpose' (Leadership Trust Foundation)
- Leaders - even those born with innate leadership talents - need to be continually developed
- Leadership styles and the needs of followers are changing
- Leadership is a trust
- Reflection is a powerful leadership development tool
- Developing leadership wisdom takes effort, time and help from others
- Start developing leadership wisdom early in your career and never stop

CHAPTER 3

The leadership development programme in Iraq

This chapter is based on my experience of designing, leading, delivering and evaluating the pilot Deans Qualifying Programme (DQP) and its subsequent roll out to other Deans and then Heads (HQP). This was an extended leadership development programme in Iraq and the chapter draws from a case study published in Schedlitzki & Edwards (2014) as well as an article in the UK's prestigious *Sunday Times* by journalist Carly Chynoweth (2011).

❧ The context

> *'All school and college leaders face challenges but those in Iraq face more than most. Many work in buildings that have been destroyed or looted since Saddam Hussein's regime fell in 2003. Power cuts are a regular event and computer access is poor. Although the political situation has become more stable, colleges still have to contend with the needs of students returning to education after being in prison, in the army or in exile, and with religious and tribal influences. On top of these practical problems, academic staff have had few opportunities to enhance their own skills' writes Chynoweth (2011).*

It was against this background that Rawabit (Arabic meaning '*partnership*') was set up jointly in 2004 by the Iraqi Foundation for Technical Education (FTE) working with a group of Further Education colleges in the UK, the Association of Colleges and other UK bodies. The collaboration drew in funding from the British government and also UNESCO. Initially Rawabit focused on support for teaching staff but in time a demand for leadership development was identified.

In 2009 I was running a leadership programme for Principals of Further Education Colleges in England (the Principals Qualifying Programme or PQP) under the auspices of the Centre For Excellence in Leadership. One of the British participants on PQP was Iraqi-born College Principal Ali Hadawi, who was also vice-Chair of Rawabit. Ali was in discussion with Dr Mahmood Abdulhussain, the President of FTE in Iraq, and told him about the ways in which his own leadership had been positively impacted by PQP. Dr Mahmood's curiosity was aroused and he brought a group of senior advisers to the UK to investigate the PQP. I spent two days with them in London with my colleague Peter Derbyshire explaining the leadership programme and discussing how it could be contextualised for them. They seemed very interested but I heard nothing for some months. However Dr Mahmood subsequently made the decision that he wanted the programme for his country. Dr Mahmood wanted it to be a world-class, developmental, programme based on the English PQP but with sensitivity towards the context and starting point of Iraq's College Deans. It would start with a small pilot group of nine Deans who would be trained to support the wider roll out of the programme across FTE and its two sister organisations in the Iraqi region of Kurdistan. There was hope that in time it would expand to include vocational school Head teachers.

The Baghdad-based FTE worked under the Ministry of Higher Education and Dr Mahmood realised that FTE needed to change from a top-down, command and control management culture to one which was much more flexible and agile. This would allow FTE to fulfil its function of meeting the training and skills needs of local economies in Iraq. The country was emerging from wars as well as security, political and economic instabilities. Prior to

1980 Iraq had been pre-eminent regionally for training and education but the current reality was that it had declined, with educational deprivation in rural areas recording over 40% illiteracy and high drop-out rates in urban colleges and schools.

Dr Mahmood wanted a transformational shift of culture and capabilities which would positively impact the leaders of the 40 Colleges and Institutes in greater Iraq (excluding Kurdistan region) which at that time had 14,000 staff and 72,000 students. What was needed were ways of working for senior leadership which would support economic reconstruction. This was a new vision of leadership. I was to learn that some Deans had been repeatedly targeted for personal attack or assassination attempts by insurgents so the context for this change could not be more demanding. It was a divided society with fractured infrastructure. There can be very few leaders who face such a perfect storm of challenges. Dr Mahmood said 'We strongly supported DQP from the start. This is an accredited programme which is helping Deans achieve our vision to strengthen the Iraqi economy through local communities. DQP is helping professionalise our senior management", (Nelson in Schedlitzki & Edwards, 2014).

❧ The Pilot programme
I began design work on the pilot DQP. I researched heavily about leadership development in a Middle East context but quickly discovered a lack of published, academically robust material for the Arab world and especially for Iraq. I was grateful to attend a timely conference on non-Western forms of leadership wisdom at the UK's Leadership Trust.

'The first challenge was deciding how basic to make the course. "Until 2003 they had been cut off from much of the outside world academically, so things that we take for granted, such as access to international libraries, was almost non-existent," Nelson said. "We had to come in assuming

nothing. We could not assume knowledge in terms of leadership" ' writes Chynoweth (2011).

I assembled a small team to help me which included two assessors I had used on the UK programme who would validate the written assignments from the Deans, providing robust feedback on their submissions. I worked with the UK's Chartered Management Institute (I have been a Fellow of CMI for many years) to build a unique international partnership with them so that Deans who successfully graduated DQP could progress through further assessment in a 'Professional Discussion' to Chartered Manager (CMgr) status. This would meet Dr Mahmood's request for a rigorous, externally accredited programme. This was the first time this external accreditation had occurred in Iraq.

The pilot group consisted mainly of ten engineers and scientists most of whom were highly educated to PhD level (one dropped out quickly on moving to a different sector). They were eager to learn and had academic curiosity which they used to form new, lateral connections out of seemingly disparate leadership models - a skill of outstanding conceptualisation. However we found that Iraq's international isolation due to sanctions under the previous regime had led to decay in their research skills. Their personal study was affected by lack of opportunities, infrastructure and limited internet access. Libraries had been destroyed, daily power cuts were the norm and information resources we took for granted in the West were at a premium.

Some things were discovered by accident. For example, at times our Western technology would not work and on one occasion I gave up trying to show a video clip and just told the story of what was in the clip. I could have heard a pin drop. The group were totally engaged with this verbal story telling. When I asked them about that effect they explained that it was the British who had introduced Iraq to the tradition of afternoon tea and during that time they stopped work and told one another stories. I consciously integrated story-telling into the programme after that.

We also had to come to terms with facilitating learning in a culture which values not losing 'face'. This did not just include participants but I came to understand that it embraced us too. Our Iraqi friends were protecting their tutors from being embarrassed by not giving us feedback when we got things wrong. This was very kind but of course it meant that I could continue for some time down a wrong track or incorrect assumption about how leadership worked in Iraq. A turning point came towards the end of the pilot, after trust and openness had increased, when an incorrect statement I had made about patriarchal leadership was gently corrected by the group leader. My initial internal reaction was a little defensive but I told myself to breathe deeply and listen carefully, realising that something special was happening. Feedback had moved into the public space and so I thanked the speaker and made a point of signalling that this was valued. This incident plays to a wider point because the Deans' environment was one in which survival meant that people had learned to keep their heads down. It had not been a safe country in which to speak your mind - sometimes not even in a family setting. We focused on helping Deans increase the validity of feedback loops. They had never asked for feedback from a subordinate and certainly not from a customer or their line manager. This was breaking new ground and so we only asked them to make small steps initially. Over time we were able to increase our level of challenge. Tutor Dave Peel reflected:

'We held in tension the need to adopt and role-model a style of coaching which was supportive and challenging whilst not reinforcing patriarchal dependency. To do this needed us to reflect on and adapt our approach. The Deans were great teachers in this endeavour and allowed us to learn through real practice with them, always seeking the wisdom in what

we were doing and how this could positively affect the hearts and minds of those who they lead.'

(Nelson in Schedlitzki & Edwards, 2014)

We noticed that feedback, even in high trust Iraqi groups, was biased towards discussion of the positives and against anything seen as negative. What sometimes helped was reframing developmental feedback to start with 'It might be even better if....' Feedback was generally of higher quality in small groups or pairs and much less so in big groups which included people who were not well known to all.

◆ The Content of DQP
The programme included:
- Taught modules to impart knowledge in high performance culture, leadership of change, engaging with external stakeholders, innovation, motivation and coaching skills
- An experiential learning workshop to help participants strengthen their peer feedback skills and raise self-awareness of their personal impact
- A 360 degree leadership feedback instrument
- A week's leadership study visit to a UK college
- A change project chosen by the participant and managed in their workplace
- A personal leadership development plan
- A 5000 word written assignment towards the end of the programme which reflected on their applied personal leadership learning, assessed on the pilot by former assessors of the English Principal's programme and on the main programmes by trained Iraqi assessors
- Written assessment for membership of CMI, to their usual UK standards
- A rigorous four hour face to face interview with an external

CMI assessor looking at 'Managing People' and 'Leading Change' competences for Chartered Manager (CMgr) status, with triangulated evidence from peers

The programme's objectives were to equip participants to understand and apply strategic leadership to improve the effectiveness of their institution and its position in the market and community. They would achieve that by understanding the impact they made as a leader; evidencing their adaptive leadership of change; developing reflective capacity; and creating a community of leadership practice.

Almost none of this was familiar to the participants. The content was new to them and the style of delivery and learning was unfamiliar. Their previous learning had been didactic and delivered from the front by an 'expert' who imparted the correct answers but DQP was designed differently to introduce learner-centred delivery. In order to be useful learning I made connections to Iraqi culture and Islamic belief and wisdom at every opportunity. Erbil, where we were delivering in Iraq, has the oldest continuously inhabited citadel settlement in the world and I frequently made connections to this unique heritage in Iraq.

I contextualised for my Iraqi Arab, and later Kurdish, audience. Some of this contextualisation took place in my research phase before the first module of the pilot but after that my programme team and I joined the class too! We had to make sense of what was happening both around us and within the group of Deans. This meant that programme design became a work in progress with our tutor's reflections leading to improvements for the next module as well as later phases of rollout. We were all learning. The pilot ran for 18 months from 2009 and we trained a cadre of Iraqi coaches and assessors able to support UK facilitators in the next phases of DQP which embraced a further 36 senior Deans in Colleges and Head Teachers in vocational Schools between 2011 and 2013.

❧ Leadership dimensions explored in Iraqi groups

I am not aware of any published leadership profile which has used a 360 degree feedback tool for Iraqi leaders. In the DQP and HQP programmes we used a leadership profiling instrument called The *Leadership Audit* which provided 360 degree feedback to each delegate. This is a proven, online process which is relatively easy to use. It focuses on areas for development which were in line with the programme's approach to leadership. The *Leadership Audit* is the Leadership Trust's web-based instrument for diagnosing the leadership strengths and development needs of leaders. The Leadership Trust is a UK charity specialising in developing leadership. The *Leadership Audit* questionnaire comprises 79 items, typically taking 20-30 minutes to complete electronically. An individual is rated on each item on a seven-point scale on the extent to which the item applies to him or her, with a provision for don't know and not applicable. The 79 items are categorised into 12 leadership and leadership-related factors:

1. Vision and mission
2. Strategy
3. Empowerment of others
4. Motivation and inspiration of others
5. Communication with others
6. Emotional intelligence
7. Team leadership
8. Coaching and mentoring others
9. Management
10. Problem solving and decision making
11. Organisational change
12. Leadership effectiveness and satisfaction

360° assessment is a process of self and stakeholder assessment of a person's leadership behaviours. It includes scoring from one's manager (boss), direct reports, peers and external contacts and is a measure of perception. The scoring can lead to useful insights on what is most important to those giving the score. 360° feedback is essentially holding up a mirror to help individuals see themselves more clearly and can be an aid to increasing self-awareness. It is however only a snapshot in time and needs to be interpreted with the help of an experienced coach. It is not a pass/fail assessment but is rather a developmental tool.

The 360° data on the programme was collected once, typically towards the start of the delegate's participation in the programme. Sadly we did not have the funding to undertake a repeat of the research to view results after programme completion. Individual profiles have been anonymised to provide an overview of the leadership summary profile of the Iraqi cohorts. There were 35 data sets (from 2010-2012) from DQP delegates and 10 data sets (2012) from HQP delegates.

❧ Summary Profile
Highest scoring leadership factors were:

Factor	HQP	DQP
Vision & Mission	82	82
Coaching & Mentoring	82	81
Management	84	80
Team Leadership	85	80
Problem Solving	79	79
Communication	83	78
Leadership Effectiveness	82	82

Lowest scoring leadership factors were:

Factor	HQP	DQP
Organisational Change	67	63
Strategy	74	72
Motivation	74	72
Empowerment	74	71
Emotional Intelligence	74	70

There was unexpected synergy between the three cohorts. The lowest scoring factors were unsurprising given the history and context of Technical Education in Iraq and confirmed the relevance of the content of DQP and HQP to help participants strengthen their effectiveness in these areas.

❧ Evaluation

Dr Moneer Tolephih, then dean of Baghdad Technical College, interviewed for a *Sunday Times* article, said that the organisational culture in colleges deferred to the Dean who was expected to make decisions on activities, or at least be consulted on them. However, after completing DQP he focused on changing the prevailing culture through coaching his team members to step up and take more of these decisions themselves. Dr Moneer said:

> *"My main challenge now is how to adapt the tools and techniques I learnt on the programme and to make sure that my leadership team is qualified to adopt them."*

> *(Chynoweth, 2011)*

∾ Outcomes

This section covers the wider roll out which took place in November 2011 for cohort two of 26 Deans and Vice Deans (including the first female Dean). This cohort embraced delegates from across the whole of Iraq including Iraqi Kurdistan, involving all three FTE's in the country. A third cohort commenced in July 2012 of ten Head Teachers of vocational schools (including three females). The programmes were designed to support participants in achieving their personal learning outcomes and to evidence their applied leadership learning. A three level model was devised when it became evident that most Deans needed to move out of description of theory to evidencing the impact they made at work. Level 1 was basic understanding of DQP material and theory (i.e. descriptive); Level 2 was thorough understanding (reflecting on applied practice); and Level 3 was adaptation and modification of that understanding. The main outcomes of the programme were:

DQP outcome (n=9) Pilot phase	Achieved	Notes
Fellowship of CMI	9	
Membership of CMI	n/a	
Graduation of DQP after written assignment	9	
Chartered Manager status	9	
DQP outcome (n=26)	Achieved	Notes
Fellowship of CMI	14	
Membership of CMI	12	

Graduation of DQP after written assignment	24 (17 at Merit,7 at Pass)	1 withdrew 1 did not complete
Chartered Manager status	24	
HQP outcome (n=10)	Achieved	
Fellowship of CMI	6	
Membership of CMI	4	
Graduation of DQP after written assignment	10 (5 at Merit, 5 at Pass)	
Chartered Manager status	10	

◈ **CMI Assessment and examples of impact on organisations**
Two assessors from CMI undertook the face to face Professional Discussions in Istanbul during which they triangulated evidence submitted by participants (including their 5000 word assignments) so as to reflect the unique setting and challenges they faced. Deans shared their personal leadership stories of how they had created business impact by:

> 'de-politicising their learning institutions; stabilising local communities through vocational education amongst former insurgents and prisoners; introducing new vocational and academic qualifications to Masters/PhD level; rebuilding Colleges destroyed in terrorist activity.
>
> (Assessor) Gaynor commented, "The most impressive stories were those of rebuilding the human soul." '

(Nelson in Schedlitzki & Edwards, 2014)

Assessor Gaynor Thomas said 'We learned so much about what is happening in Iraq and the leadership and management Deans have had to exhibit in such very complex and difficult circumstances. What they have achieved is most impressive and it was very clear how they had successfully applied the models and concepts learned on the DQP in their Institutes, which have successfully blossomed under their leadership', (Nelson, 2011c).

An analysis of the change projects undertaken by the 34 successful graduates of the second and third programmes showed the primary aims of their Change Projects included:

- Improving teaching & learning including curriculum changes to increase employability
- Management Team development
- Improving infrastructure including new laboratories and iT
- Changing the organisational culture including de-politicising campus
- Increasing student numbers
- Improving stakeholder partnerships including reputation for local economic development
- Raising organisational performance
- Increasing non-government revenue
- Personal change as a leader
- Strategy development

Analysis of both written assignments and Professional Discussion documents revealed that 'there were 61 sustainable new employer relationships developed. This is compelling evidence that the programme stimulated an outward-facing leadership mindset focused on meeting the needs of external stakeholders. It also developed internal organisational capacity and capability....Most Head Teachers chose a project primarily focused on the students whereas Deans tended to engage with a broader range of strategic choices' (Nelson, 2011c).

Anonymised comments (Nelson, 2011c) from participants include:

> *'Instead of seeing inadequate funding in negative terms I saw it as an opportunity to identify and implement changes. There was demand amongst employed workers to gain qualifications. I introduced a new pattern of student attendance. This meant the resources of the department are now fully used instead of standing idle; it has provided career developmental opportunities to employees undertaking the programme and has given my department a new source of revenue'.*

One participant told the story of how, faced with insufficient resources to fund the build of a new laboratory, he formed a team to look at how to build their own lab. The team reverse-engineered a solution using a defunct facility. His doubts about whether the plan would work were unfounded as he saw this high performing team work with him during their own time off on the major holiday of Eid to achieve the task.

> *'I have developed criteria to determine the progress of the institution. Performance indicators for all employees have been introduced'*

Another DQP graduate used SWOT analysis to identify an opportunity in the local economy which produces almonds and pomegranates. Production was limited and seasonal and the College realised that it had expertise which could assist the producers expand their growing windows. A team of lecturers, students and local producers was established to look at ways to help the producers harness new markets. 65 students are now working on this team and they are often being recruited on completion of their studies.

An HQP graduate explained that people were initially reluctant to express their views openly but as he worked on trust the feedback increased. This led to a review of the prices in the canteen when it became known that students from poor backgrounds could not afford to eat there. This resulted in those students having *'more energy during the day, concentrating better at their studies and enjoying life at school a lot more'.*

❧ Examples of impact on personal leadership practice
Anonymised comments (Nelson, 2011c) included:

'Through DQP I have learnt how powerful coaching is as a technique in the leadership of people'.

A delegate said that they now empower and delegate as much as they can as they understand that their staff are the experts in their field. He gives them space to complete tasks but ensures they know that he is available for support if needed. He focuses on the people issues and reflects *'It is interesting that one often sees managers spending time to ensure that light bulbs are changed and are all working but they spend less time working on those people who are broken and not functioning well.'*

A Head observed *'I have learned more about leadership in HQP than in over 20 years as a Head Teacher. I used to shake with fear but now I am confident.'*

A DQP graduate described his involvement of the security guards to resolve a problem with the way patrols were carried out. In the past solutions were always dictated from senior management but this different approach resulted in a better, more innovative outcome with greater ownership of their new routines and training.

'I surveyed former students and asked how they we could develop our curriculum and they identified skills and knowledge which would have eased their transfer into work. When they started work

they were being asked to operate machinery and equipment they had no knowledge of. I identified opportunities to ensure our students leave us skilled in modern techniques.'

One Dean admitted to seeing feedback as negative criticism but had reframed it into a learning opportunity. They had, for example, acted on feedback about their teaching style and changed their delivery pace in response. They are encouraging feedback for other members of staff to help them identify other improvements. The Dean is also seeking feedback on his performance from a wide range of internal and external stakeholders.

❧ Other personal impacts

One Dean (Nelson, 2011c) said DQP 'was an injection of energy to boost our hopes and dreams and gave us the opportunity to forget a lot of the worries that have accompanied our work throughout the dark period that we went through'.

Another Dean had to work firstly to restore the Institute which had lacked the most basic supplies needed to sustain its role, and secondly to rehabilitate the 'infected human soul' which was destroyed by what had happened. The first task he says was rather easy, but the second task was much more difficult to achieve. 'What had happened in our country resulted in people lacking trust or faith in any leader; they were accustomed to the bureaucratic officials who are chasing after their own interests... The majority of workers who had suffered the frustrations of the past have found it difficult to improve.....I have been able to help them change by restoring their confidence in management, by encouraging them and rewarding their achievements'. He reflected on his learning that management of people in unstable circumstances such as Iraq was extremely difficult, (Nelson, 2011c).

The evidence from delegates in the wider roll out demonstrated significant impact reaching up to level 4 of the Kirkpatrick (1996) model for evaluating training interventions. It is generally accepted that being able to evidence impact at Level 4 is very unusual.

Kirkpatrick levels

Level 4: Results	To what degree targeted outcomes occur, as a result of the learning event(s) and subsequent reinforcement.
Level 3: Behaviour	To what degree participants apply what they learned during training when they are back on the job.
Level 2: Learning	To what degree participants acquire the intended knowledge, skills, and attitudes based on their participation in the learning event.
Level 1: Reaction	To what degree participants react favourably to the learning event.

❧ Reflections on the programme

I learned as programme director to be more flexible and not to be too restricted by the planning I had done before each module. It was often necessary to work 'in the moment' because that was how Iraqi culture worked. At any time for example we might have a visit from a V.I.P to one of our workshops in Erbil or Sulaymaniyah and when that happened delivery was interrupted. Sometime Iraqi media would arrive, having been invited by our Iraqi hosts, and would want to film our proceedings and conduct interviews for TV or radio whilst we were continuing with delivery. I continually learned deeper meanings of Insha'Allah.

Delivery took more time than it would with a UK group and that had to be factored in to the workshop design. This was partly because of the need for simultaneous translation into Arabic and Kurdish but also because participants needed time to absorb and process new concepts. This meant adjustments to pace, style and content. UK humour and colloquial terms did not travel. We found that groups work very differently in Iraq and typically there is a higher level of collaboration than in an English Principals' group, which would show greater individual competition. There was a constant search for the 'wisdom' in our activities, lectures and even any ice-breaker exercises we used. This search for wisdom was always undertaken as a group activity in Iraq rather than as an individual take-away.

❧ Conclusions and the future

The pilot achieved its aim of building a group of Iraqi leaders able to support wider rollout and assessment. All participants in the pilot achieved the triple award of DQP, FCMI and CMgr. The standards for assessment and leadership were customised and contextualised but never diluted. The two subsequent cohorts of DQP and HQP equipped participants with continuous and sustainable improvement in their personal leadership skills, knowledge and impact. Customised Leadership Standards were developed for use by Iraqi FTE. All but two participants in phase 2 and 3 achieved the triple award of DQP, FCMI/MCMI and CMgr.

The success of DQP came by building strong and trusting relationships to enable partnership. The applied leadership wisdom from DQP and HQP is helping FTE and its sister bodies shape a generation of senior leaders; impact the whole Technical Education system over time; and strengthen economic and social gains. These all add up to being a 'perfect pearl' (*al-Jiwan*) for Technical education in Iraq. A decade after its pilot launch in 2009 the work of leadership development and coaching continues as a largely Iraqi-led series of interventions. The DQP/HQP programmes helped Iraqi senior leaders in Technical Colleges (many now have the status of Technical Universities) and vocational schools to change the leadership culture of their organisations and institutions. They have taken ownership of their professional leadership development and this continued in the face of the invasion from Daesh and ongoing political and economic instability. Between 2016 and 2018, for example, in a programme in partnership with UNESCO and the

British Council, the leadership coaches and trainers from DQP and HQP supported intensive capacity building work with 100 leaders across Iraq and undertook a leadership Training Needs Analysis for a larger group of managers (British Council, 2018). The DQP and HQP graduates are continuing to apply the lessons learned in their day to day leadership practice impacting thousands of students and staff along with their local economies.

'Whoever works any act of Righteousness and has Faith – his endeavour will not be rejected. We shall record it in his favour'

(Qur'an 21: 94)

ᘒ Key Wisdom in this chapter
- Western leadership concepts and models need adaptation and contextualisation for an Islamic audience
- Story telling is a powerful learning vehicle
- Building trust is essential in a Middle East context as no learning will occur without it - but it takes time
- It takes even more time for people to be ready to share the gift of high quality personal feedback
- Western leadership development consultants need to become comfortable working 'in the moment'
- Groups will work together to find 'the wisdom' in activities
- Leadership development can have a significant impact on leaders individually, the teams they lead, their organisations and communities they serve

CHAPTER 4

Leadership wisdom from the Prophet Muhammad ﷺ

By Professor Moneer Hameed Tolephih Ph.D.,
President of the University of Baghdad, Iraq

'On a journey the leader of a people is their servant'

(Prophet Muhammad quoted in Adair, 2010)

Muslim and non-Muslim historians have written many books about the Prophet Muhammad as a leader, highlighting the divinely guided qualities of his personality. But in the past century or so, a modernist, rationalist school of Islamic thought has emerged, which focuses on examining Prophet Muhammad as a charismatic leader as well as being the messenger of God (the Prophet). The Prophet Muhammad was a statesman, a businessman, a political leader and a spiritual guide. This case study does not try to examine the miraculous nature of the Prophet's biography but rather explores the rationalist and humanist dimensions of his personality as an extraordinary leader. It is this examination as a role model leader which uncovers wisdom for leadership in his life. This is wisdom which we can follow in our own practice of leadership.

There are more than 400 books and research studies (including at PhD. and MSc. levels) in western countries studying the leadership and management concepts of the Prophet Muhammad. A Google search on this topic produces 3.9m returns globally. There is considerable interest in the lessons for leadership from his extraordinary life.

᠃᠊᠊᠊᠊᠊᠊᠊᠊ **Key highlights from the Prophet's life:**
- Prophet Muhammad was born on April 22, 571 AD at Mecca.
- **Birth and upbringing:** Muhammad's father died before he was born and he was raised first by his grandfather and then by his uncle (Abu Talib). His mother died when he was four years of age.
- **Muhammad's life:** Muhammad through his life practiced many jobs as a shepherd and working in commerce; he was famous for his honesty, sincerity and wisdom.
- **Prophetic mission:** when he was 40 years old, he started the prophetic mission which lasted until his death 23 years later.
- **Migration to Medina:** through his prophetic mission and due to the vexation of 'Qurraish' (local Mecca citizens), Muhammad (pbuh) managed to migrate to Medina which was far enough away (450 km) to allow the first steps to establish the Islamic state.
- **Islamic state-building:** Muhammad from the first day of migration started to build the Islamic state through many state values, such as supporting education, work, brotherhood of migrants with Medina citizens, ethics, women's rights and by showing peace to neighbours of Islam. He built many peace agreements with Medina neighbors.
- **The Conquest of Mecca:** This was achieved in 630 AD through a peaceful agreement.
- **Islamic conquests:** It was made a condition that the Islamic state will not attack any neighbors unless it had been attacked by them, i.e. it would only be for defensive action, but at the same time Muhammad sent representatives to many cities and civilizations to invite them to choose Islam.

❧ The leader as a Shepherd

There is power in using metaphors, such as when comparing leaders to shepherds. The adjectives that come to mind include humility and courage. A good shepherd can be seen to guide his sheep, unite them and work for their welfare without taking advantage of them. The shepherd cares for each individual sheep. 'The biblical image of the shepherd well illustrates (the) threefold responsibility for meeting task, team and individual needs... the shepherd provides direction, maintains the unity of the flock and meets the individual needs of the sheep' (Adair, 1989). Those characteristics were evidenced in the life and actions of Prophet Muhammad - he cared for the well-being of each and every member of his flock. The Prophet describes each member of the Muslim community as a shepherd and guardian:

Prophet Muhammad explains the exchangeable responsibility between the leader and his follower:

' *"Beware every one of you is a shepherd and every one is answerable with regard to his flock". The Caliph is a shepherd over the people and he shall be questioned about his subjects (as to how he conducted their affairs). A man is a guardian over the members of his family and shall be questioned about them (as to how he looked after their physical and moral well-being). A woman is a guardian over the household of her husband and his children and shall be questioned about them'*

(narrated on the authority of Ibn 'Umar; Sahih Muslim 1829a Book 33, Hadith 24) in 'Leadership and Islam' Ali, A. (p87), Metcalfe and Mimouni, (2001)

❧ Honest, trustworthy and wise

One of the main qualities of the Prophet Muhammad was known before the Prophet's mission. He was a treasurer of money to Quraish and the leader of commercial caravans, so he gained an excellent reputation for his honesty and trustworthiness. In addition, Muhammad was known in Mecca society for his deep thinking and wisdom, where he offered many solutions of critical cases and avoided possible conflict amongst his people. As an example, the Kaaba in Mecca was exposed to the action of the rains which led to the removal of the Black Stone (holy stone) and caused cracks in the stones of Kaaba. After rebuilding the Kaaba, the tribes argued over who would restore the Black Stone to its original position. Every tribe wanted to do it and it became a critical issue likely to cause a fight. Muhammad used wisdom and deep thinking to solve the issue by making all of the tribes participate in the return of the Black Stone. It was placed on Mohammad's cloak and raised by all at the same time, and then Muhammad put it onto its position. Everyone was satisfied with the solution. This is an example of the leader using critical thinking to solve a critical problem.

ᴄᴥ Hijra - the emigration to Medina

Emigration to Medina marked a turning point in the life of the Prophet Muhammad, peace be upon him, as well as in the history of Islam. It is illuminating to look at the reasons the Prophet Muhammad chose Medina as the place to migrate to:

- Arabic was spoken in Medina unlike the alternative of Abyssinia
- It was a nearer location than Abyssinia, making it easier for older Muslims to reach
- The Prophet led the negotiations with the leaders and representatives of Medina for the reception of immigrants after the era of Aqaba
- Prophet Muhammad in his search for a safe place went to Taif (Thaqeef), but he did not succeed there in spite of the unity of language so he exchanged Taif with Medina as his chosen location

- The distance between Mecca and Medina is 450 km and it was therefore far enough away from the infidel enemy at Mecca.

Consideration of the above points shows that Muhammad analysed them in terms of their strengths, weakness, opportunity and threats. In modern management theory this is known as a SWOT analysis method, so it is clear that Muhammad made his decision for emigration to Medina on a logical and scientific basis. The approach that Muhammad adopted illustrates his depth of thinking and wisdom of his decision as a leader.

∾ Covenants and agreements

Prophet Muhammad initiated a peaceful political step on the platform being built for the Islamic faith by drawing up a document of peace and non-aggression, which described rights and duties between Muslims and Jews in Medina. The document was a charter for peace, security and coexistence between these parties and was established in the light of justice and understanding to identify mutual rights and obligations. The reader is invited to reflect on these Strengths, Weaknesses, Opportunities and Threats (SWOT) questions on the basis of the emigration to Medina.

STRENGTHS	WEAKNESSES
What were the strengths of the choice of Medina for emigration?	What were the weakest points of the choice of Medina for the emigration?
OPPORTUNITIES	THREATS
What were the opportunities in the choice of Medina for emigration?	What were the threats in the choice of Medina for emigration?

Through all the battles fought by the Prophet Muhammad, he effectively adopted the basics of SWOT analysis. Prophet Muhammad discussed with his companions the points of strength in the field during the battle, including the number of soldiers; locations and strategic plans; various weaknesses; how to develop plans in mitigation; victory as an opportunity and the multiple threats to the army or community. As an example, in the Uhud battle Muhammad responded to the difference in the numbers of both sides by choosing a suitable battlefield, and used the geography of the land to overcome the shortfall in the number of his fighters. Muhammad used the mountains for supporting locations. Initially the Muslims won the battle but due to the withdrawal of many fighters, Muslims eventually lost the battle. Muhammad as a leader drew many lessons from that event (in reflection) and shared them with companions for future use.

ꙮ Muhammad's leadership skills

Prophet Muhammad was a good listener to all of his companions and other people, paying attention to Muslims (including young people and women) and even infidels. Prophet Muhammad looked out for the safety of his companions from the earliest days of his mission. For example, to spare his followers the risk of persecution he arranged for them to migrate to Abyssinia for their safety. Their welfare was uppermost in his mind. Prophet Muhammad joked with his companions and built bridges of understanding and trust - he was only severe with those who attacked the strategic values of the state or of Islam. Prophet Muhammad was an example of courage - when he was in the battlefield he lifted his companions' morale and reinforced in their minds noble values and he was the last to withdraw. Prophet Muhammad was involved with his companions in daily work tasks and he refused to let others do the work instead of him.

Prophet Muhammad was not above listening to advice from his younger subordinates or companions, for example in the battle of the Trench (Al-Khandak):

'It is true that most of the Muslims were terror-stricken but there was one among them who was not. He had, in fact, volunteered to accept Amr's very first challenge but the Prophet had restrained him, hoping that someone else might like to face him (Amr). But he could see that no one dared to measure swords with him.

The young man who was willing to take up Amr's challenge was no one other than Ali ibn Abi Talib, the hero of Islam. When Amr hurled his third challenge, and no one answered him, Ali rose and solicited the Prophet's permission to go out and to fight against him. The Prophet of Islam had no choice now but to allow his cousin, Ali, the Lion of Islam, to go and to silence the taunts and the jibes of Amr ibn Abd Wudd.

Ali put on the battle-dress of the Prophet of Islam. The latter himself suspended the Dhu'l-Fiqar to his side, and prayed for his victory, saying: "O Allah! Thou hast called to Thy service, Obaida ibn al-Harith, on the day the battle of Badr was fought, and Hamza ibn Abdul-Muttalib, on the day the battle of Uhud was fought. Now Ali alone is left with me. Be Thou his Protector, give him victory, and bring him back safely to me."

When the Prophet saw Ali going toward his adversary, he said: "He is the embodiment of all Faith who is going to an encounter with the embodiment of all Unbelief."'

(Al-Islam, 2019)

Prophet Muhammad was open to advice – for example he took strategic action through digging a trench around the battle field to overcome the enemy in response to advice received from his Persian companion Salman.

Prophet Muhammad made correct assessments for the tasks entrusted to his companions. He valued the feedback process. In the liberation of Mecca one of the companions (Sahabah) said that on that epic day they should take women captive but the Prophet Muhammad replied 'today is the day of mercy and preserving the dignity of women'. Prophet Muhammad, whenever he left Medina, delegated his representative with full authority to lead in his absence, demonstrating a high degree of trust.

❧ Muhammad and high performance teams

Muhammad was able to build a high performance leadership team by choosing as companions role models such as Abu Bakr, Umar Bin Alkhatab, Uthman Bin Affan and Ali bin Abe Talib. Those companions and some others started their Islamic journey close to Muhammad. He prepared and qualified them to fill the expected roles for the team. Those selected companions had different abilities such as courage, honesty, sincerity, humility, patience and faith in the prophetic mission. The performance of the companions, through the team led by Muhammad, reflected well on the subsequent building of the Islamic state, which faced great and fateful challenges. Muhammad shepherded the companions with advice and guidance, noble values and Islamic ideas in order to develop them to become distinctive role models for influencing Islamic society.

❧ How the Prophet Muhammad chose people for posts

Muhammad was unique in discovering promising and competent people in his community and appointing them to the work they could do best. Muhammad planned to spread the message of Islam beyond Arabia. He decided to write to neighbouring kings, including those of the super powers, inviting them to consider Islam. In selecting the best ambassadors to travel to kings and heads of state, Prophet Muhammad chose some of the most competent of his companions. These ambassadors were conversant with the languages spoken as well as with the political conditions of the countries to which they were sent; they were qualified in the holy Qur'an and the philosophy of Islam.

❧ Prophet's wisdom in leading his country
An Islamic leader gains the love and trust of his people and is followed by them in proportion to his competence in solving their problems. This may include issues which are personal, public, social, economic, political or touching the community as a whole. The Prophet Muhammad exemplified leadership which addressed all of these aspects.

❧ Equality and Brotherhood of Man
Prophet Muhammad acknowledged the equality and brotherhood of man. He was not content with just preaching it - he practiced it. One of his closest companions was a former Negro slave, Bilaal; one of his trusted lieutenants was an Iranian called Salmaan; a third, Suhayb of Rome. These followers came from different places, spoke different languages and were of different heritage. However, in their teacher's school, they were treated the same and were equal to each other. Immediately after his settlement in Medina, Prophet Muhammad, peace be upon him, established brotherhood between Muslims, particularly between the emigrants and the helpers (Medina citizen). They loved each other and were very close to each other. For example, Sa'd ibn Rabi' took his emigrant 'brother' 'Abd al-Rahman ibn 'Awf to his house and said: 'Brother, you have left everything you have in Mecca. So, this house, with everything in it, belongs to both of us. (Qur'an 50:50).

❧ Companions felt safe with the Prophet Muhammad
Narrated by Mu'adh ibn Jabal:

> *'The Messenger of Allah said: if anyone suppresses anger when he is in a position to give vent to it Allah, the exalted,*

will call him on the day of resurrection over the heads of all creatures, and ask him to choose any of the bright and large-eyed maidens he wishes.'

Abu Dawud said: the name of the transmitter Abu Marham is 'Abd Al-Rahman b. Maimun

Grade Hasan (Al Albani)
Reference: Sunan Abi Dawud 4777
English translation: Book 42, Hadith 4759

The Prophet worked to help people feel safe as evidenced in the liberation of Mecca and the Prophet's forgiveness of its non-Muslim citizens. Muhammad showed great forgiveness of the offending neighbours.

◝ Prophet Muhammad used consultations

The Prophet was committed to the use of consultation and was guided by the Quranic verse:

'It is part of the mercy of Allah that thou dost deal gently with them. Wert thou severe or harsh-hearted, they would have broken away from about thee: so pass over (their faults), and ask for (Allah's) forgiveness for them; and consult them in affairs (of moment). Then, when thou hast taken a decision, put thy trust in Allah. For Allah loves those who put their trust (in Him).

(Qur'an, Al 'Imran, 3:159)

Prophet Muhammad before the battle of Badr consulted with the Companions:

'He consulted with his Companions before Badr, the first major post-Emigration military encounter, about whether the Muslims

should fight the approaching Meccan army. The Muslim forces numbered 305 or 313, while the Meccans numbered around
one thousand. As mentioned, one spokesman each for the Emigrants and the Helpers stood up and proclaimed their readiness
to follow him wherever he might lead them. During his life, all
Companions continually promised to follow him in every step he
took, and to carry out all of his orders. Despite this, the Messenger consulted with them about almost every community-wide
matter so that this practice would become second nature'.

(Infinite Light, 2019)

The Prophet listened to the wise words of Sa'ad ibn Mu'adh:

'After the Prophet migrated to Medinah, after being reas-
sured by Sa'ad and his Companions from the Ansaar (helper) about his victory and the victory of Islam, Sa'ad had the
stance of men who have been true to what they have vowed
before Allah. It was those positions when the Muslims took
to the Battle of Badr to meet the infidels, when the Prophet
consulted the Ansaar (helper).

Sa'ad said: "We believe in you, we declare your truth, and we
witness that what you have brought us is the truth and we
have given you our word and agreement to hear and obey, so
go where you wish, we are with you; and by He (God) who
sent you, if you were to ask us to cross this sea and you plunged
into it, we would plunge into it with you; not a man would
stay behind. We do not dislike the idea of meeting our enemy
tomorrow. We are experienced in war, capable of fighting. It
may well be that Allah will let us show you something which
will bring you joy, so take us along with Allah's blessing.'

(Al- Muhajir, 2017)

༄ Prophet Mohammad paid attention
to the Alsahaba and community

Prophet Muhammad asked the prisoners taken in the battle of Badr to teach ten Muslims to read and write in order to gain their liberty. The Prophet knew that this would develop and improve the capabilities of Muslims as well as enhance their skills and competencies. After that those prisoners lived with the Muslims for more than six months and learned much about Islam and some of them decided to become a Muslim through studying their beliefs.

༄ Muhammad and Ethics

The Prophet focused on demonstrating in practical ways the core values of Islam, for example, when he kissed the hands of a worker who worked hard, and he said "This hand be loved by God and Prophet", (Saheh Muslim).

> *An effective leader in the Islamic sense is firmly grounded in a strong ethical foundation that guides all his or her activities or thinking'*

> *Metcalfe and Murfin (in Metcalfe and Mimouni, 2011)*

Ikrimah ibn Abi Jahl was one of the worst enemies of the prophet Muhammad, peace be upon him. There was an occasion when he hurt his companions with gross abuse. He was one of the powerful leaders of Mecca, the first and major Sheik, but Prophet Mohammad asked the community to welcome Ikrimah and forgive him:

> *'Ikrimah said "I ask you to ask God for forgiveness for me for all the hostility I directed against you and for whatever insults I expressed in your presence or absence." The Prophet replied with the prayer: "O Lord, forgive him for all the*

hostility he directed against me and for all the expeditions he mounted wishing to put out Your light. Forgive him for whatever he has said or done in my presence or absence to dishonour me."

Ikrimah's face beamed with happiness. "By God, O messenger of Allah, I promise that whatever I have spent obstructing the way of God, I shall spend twice as much in His path and whatever battles I have fought against God's way I shall fight twice as much in His way."

From that day on, Ikrimah was committed to the mission of Islam as a brave horseman in the field of battle and as a steadfast worshipper who would spend much time in mosques reading the book of God. Often he would place the mushaf on his face and say, "The Book of my Lord, the words of my Lord" and he would cry from the fear of God'.

(Islamic Centre of Redmond, 2019)

ꙮ Muhammad's political leadership

The prophet's political leadership was successful. The Prophet had confidence in victory and in his behaviours he 'practiced what he preached'. The Prophet worked to ensure understanding and called for commitment from the Companions. He showed his leadership ability in dealing with new respondents to the invitation to believe. He encouraged complete trust between his followers and Muhammad had great ability to recognize and release the potential in followers. The Prophet could solve urgent problems with minimum effort. Muhammad was recognized as being far-sighted and showed leadership based on the reality of situations. The Prophet had the ability to control nation-building, making it unified and able to withstand the pressures of long-term growth.

❧ Key Wisdom in this chapter

- At the close of this chapter, we can state many conclusions about leadership of Muhammad ﷺ:

- Muhammad showed people distinctive and excellent behaviors such as honesty and integrity, which enhanced their confidence in his personality.

- He respected everyone and showed them compassion and offered cooperation.

- He listened to advice and consulted with companions during important decisions.

- He created a team of companions to be leaders in the Muslim community and developed them as role models.

- He contributed to the promotion of the noblest values in society, and he used them in the Islamic invitation (Da'wa).

- As a leader, he left a competent representative when leaving Medina and delegated to him all the power he needed to run Medina. When a representative was dispatched on any mission he checked the selection of the most competent and appropriate person.

- He gave value and status to women in society ensuring they were treated with dignity.

- There are several examples of where Muhammad used SWOT analysis, explicitly or indirectly, to help make a substantive decision.

- Muhammad completed many agreements with neighboring cities and civilizations to organize relations and build common bonds.

- Muhammad as a leader focused on foundational concepts like justice, equality, honesty, sincerity, humility and noble values, in order to build a civilized society.

CHAPTER 5

An overview of key Leadership Theories

The reader is introduced to a range of leadership paradigms (ways to view a subject) and theories in order to stimulate thinking about leadership. This chapter is not a complete guide to leadership theory but covers the main themes and movements. It will help the reader in their own leadership journey by providing some theoretical underpinning as shared on the DQP and HQP programmes. The chapter presents some of the key leadership theories that have contributed to our evolving understanding of leadership today and some of the theorists who have prompted this development. This chapter contains some parts originally written for an unpublished guide to leadership theory for DQP and HQP participants, edited by the author (Nelson, 2012).

'The study of leadership rivals in age the emergence of civilisation, which shaped its leaders as much as it was shaped by them. From its infancy, the study of history has been the study of leaders – what they did and why they did it'

(Bass, 1990b)

Leadership influences every aspect of organisational performance (Fiedler, 1967) and its effectiveness is crucial to explain or predict organisational performance (Bennis and Nanus, 1985; Yukl, 1998). Leadership ultimately influences the outcomes of all organisational performance (Jaffee, 2001; Andersen, 2000).

In an online video lecture Adair (2016) described what he called the 'universal body of knowledge' (or practical wisdom) about leadership. Adair identified three streams: a Western stream, drawing on Greek and Roman thinking; an Eastern stream, which includes writers such as Confucius; and a Tribal stream. Adair (2010) writes 'all humankind has passed – or is passing – through a period when the dominant institution of society is the tribe. This fact has given us innate preferences for certain characteristics in our leaders. We expect them, if they are to fulfil the generic role of leader, to be both competent and benevolent'. Adair explains that tribal tradition's wisdom has been passed down from generation to generation, often in proverbs. Adair sees each of these streams as relevant to understand the 'jigsaw puzzle' of leadership.

Schedlitzki and Edwards (2014) categorised 'traditional' approaches to leadership into four main headings which I have used below to help the reader grasp an overview of both classical influences and modern developments in the study of leadership. Inevitably this is weighted towards the Western voice and research for reasons explained earlier in this book but I have added specific insights from my research on leadership in Middle East and/or Islamic contexts.

❧ THEME 1: The study of leadership and management

How Leadership and Management relate

Kotter (1990) articulated the disagreement as to how leadership relates to management, where the two overlap and whether the two are distinct phenomena (Yukl, 1998). Kotter's interpretation conceptualizes management as coping with complexity by seeking to establish order and consistency within the organisation, while leadership might be seen as producing organisational change and movement. It is possible to be a manager or a leader and some people are both. All of us have been influenced by someone who did not hold formal hierarchical authority or power over us and that is also a form of leadership. Management is often considered and taught as a science whilst leadership is often viewed as an art. While many of the most effective managers are strong leaders and many effective leaders have strong management skills, it is possible to draw a distinction between these two complementary processes.

LEADERSHIP Produces organisational movement and change	MANAGEMENT Produces organisational order and consistency
Motive and Inspire • Inspires and energises • Satisfies unmet needs • Empowers employees	**Controlling and Problem Solving** • Develop incentives • Generates creative solutions • Takes coercive action
Establishes Strategic Direction • Creates the organisational vision • Sets strategies • Clarifies big picture	**Planning and Budgeting** • Sets timetables • Allocates resources effectively • Establishes agendas
Aligning People and Organisation • Communicates goals • Builds teams and coalitions • Actively seeks commitment	**Organising and Staffing** • Provides structure • Establishes rules and procedures • Makes job placements

Figure: The Functions of Leadership and Management (Kotter, 1990) adapted

More recent leadership thinkers (Birkinshaw, 2010) have criticised distinctions made by Kotter. They see management and leadership as complementary, in effect 'two horses pulling the same cart'. We need both functions in organisations and when either one is missing problems ensue. The Management Innovation eXchange (2019) set up by Prof. Gary Hamel has initiated a deeper exploration of these themes and starts from the premise that the management models in use today are broken and inappropriate for a 21st Century world.

Leadership paradigms

One way to approach leadership theory is through the exploration of leadership paradigms. The Business Dictionary defines a paradigm as an 'intellectual perception or view, accepted by an individual or a society as a clear example, model, or pattern of how things work in the world'. Avery (2004) describes leadership paradigms by the preferred style of leading, flexibility to changing circumstances and the reaction of followers to their experience of the leader.

Taylorism paradigm

In the early twentieth century Taylor (2009) developed the theory of scientific management. An engineer by profession, Taylor blended the development of technology with a quest for efficiency, task quantification and standardisation of the industrial process. He believed the average worker was an economic unit, motivated solely by pay. Taylor's legacy to the industrialised world was the time and motion study. His thinking influenced H.L. Gantt (of Gantt chart fame) and Henry Ford who used these principles in the mass production of cars. This led to the emergence of 'Taylorism' and 'Fordism' as paradigms and they continue to exercise influence on business organisation and leadership (Goffee and Jones, 2000). The notion of organisations having leaders as opposed to managers did not emerge until later in the 20th century (Collingwood, 2001).

Hierarchy of Needs paradigm

Maslow's (1962) work on motivation influenced much leadership and management theory. He categorised human needs into a hierarchy and each category builds upon the next starting with physical needs.

The need for
self-actualisation

Experience purpose, meaning
and realising all inner potentials.

Esteen Need
The need to be a unique individual with self-respect
and to enjoy general esteem from others.

Love and belonging needs
The need for belonging, to receive and give love,
appreciation, friendship.

Security Need
The basic need for social security in a family and a society
that protects against hunger and violence.

The Physiological Needs
The need for food, water, shelter and clothing.

Figure: Adapted from Maslow (1962)

Hertzberg's Dual Factor Theory (1959) built on this work of Maslow and concluded it was possible to meet both intrinsic and extrinsic human needs at the same time. Hertzberg developed new insights into reward and motivation, distinguishing between 'hygiene factors' and 'motivators'. He noted that staff satisfaction was not equally influenced by these factors. Hygiene factors reduced dissatisfaction (they include salary and benefits, relationships with co-workers, the work environment, the supervisory style, status and security). In other words they reduced people's *unhappiness* at work but did not actually make them happy. However he found that it was motivators which actually increased satisfaction (they include recognition, self-esteem, challenge, achievement, responsibility and growth). It was motivators that created a positive feeling.

Theory X and Theory Y paradigm

McGregor (1960) argued the traditionally structured hierarchical organisation, with decision-making taken at the top, implied specific views about human nature and motivation. He named these

Theory X and Theory Y. In Theory X organisations, leadership is likely to be of an authoritarian, repressive style. With such tight control over workers' activity, development is very limited and the organisational culture will be constrained and depressed. The typical employee according to *Theory X* mindset:

- dislikes work and will avoid it if he can
- must be faced with the threat of punishment to work towards objectives
- prefers to be directed
- prefers to avoid responsibility
- is relatively unambitious, and wants security

In Theory Y organisations leadership is liberating and the approach is developmental. Control still operates in the organisation but the emphasis switches to achievement and continuous improvement. Improvement is achieved by enabling staff, empowering them and giving them responsibility. The Theory Y leader believes that the workplace should respect its workers who should be encouraged to do their best. In a *Theory Y* organisation it is believed that:

- Effort in work is as natural as play
- People will apply self-control and self-direction to achieve objectives
- People accept and seek responsibility
- The capacity to use imagination, ingenuity and creativity in solving problems is widely distributed
- Intellectual potential needs to be harnessed

McGregor's work marked a move away from authoritarian leadership where workers were treated as machines or economic units.

Classical Leadership paradigm

Leadership paradigms may be seen on a continuum between autocratic and democratic extremes (Bass, 1990a). Typically, the autocratic leader will use a command and control approach in which followers have to obey the leader's orders out of fear, obedience, respect or perhaps a belief in the leader's abilities and their right to lead. Such classical leadership provides stability for their followers (who do not have to make decisions, only implement them) but such leaders may change direction without consultation. There are occasions when a command and control style of leadership is useful, for example, in a failing organisation which has to be urgently turned around by a Chief Executive brought in to bring substantial change in a short time. Often in such cases, the formal and informal structures of the organisation have limited responsiveness to change other than by a command and control approach. However this type of leader can be perceived as ruthless and their time in leadership ends once the turnaround is achieved because a more democratic style then becomes necessary. Where Autocratic leadership becomes the cultural norm the impact on an organisation is negative. Followers are likely to become de-skilled and incapable of using their initiative. Succession of an autocratic leader is problematic - followers may hold the leader in such reverence that an incoming boss will struggle to impose his or her authority on the role. This effect can sometimes be seen in the U.K.'s Premier League after the loss of a highly autocratic football manager.

More recent leadership perspectives in Asian countries (Badawy, 1980; Reading, 1990; Whitley, 1992), Arab countries (Muna, 1980; Hofstede, 1984) and African countries (Dia, 1994) provide extensive evidence of an acceptance and legitimisation of directive and autocratic leadership styles as opposed to western leadership theories and models which generally emphasise delegation, empowerment and power sharing as key components of effective leadership. They reported that the authority of a leader is accepted as right and proper and that subordinates must show respect and obedience. Research in East Asia (Whitley, 1992), Arab countries (Muna, 1980) and Africa (Dia, 1994) reported that a leader's legitimacy and acceptance was often dependent on non-utilitarian qualities deeply rooted in culture and not performance. In these setting it was less likely that leadership would be withdrawn as a result of followers' dissatisfaction, or through a lack of technical competence (Dia, 1994).

᷎ THEME 2: **The study of individual leadership competences**

Traits and Skills theory
In an attempt to understand what makes a leader, people have for centuries tried to identify and describe characteristics or traits of successful leaders. Sun Tzu's (2009) study of leadership and strategy, *The Art of War*, was written around 500 B.C. and he identified five characteristics of a leader as one who 'must be intelligent, trustworthy, caring, brave, and strict'. Sun Tzu formed the basis for the first recorded Trait-theory of leadership. Gill (2006) argues that such non-western conceptualisations of leadership are paid little attention in modern leadership research or published journals. This is surprising given the profound nature of these writings and the long lasting effect they have had on generations of leaders. Plato (1997) in *The Republic*, c.380 B.C. argued that people best suited to lead were those with the greatest knowledge and so promoted the notion of the *philosopher king* as 'best able to guard the laws and institutions of our State-let them be our guardians'. Over time thinking about leadership has been expressed in such 'great man' theories. In *The Prince* the mediaeval writer Machiavelli (2017) described leaders in terms of their attributes. He argued that appearances were important despite the underlying motive or reality. Machiavelli wrote that the leader must appear compassionate, generous and develop through cunning the appearance of great integrity - despite actually being cruel, mean

and self-centred. To many this approach seems unacceptable and 'Machiavellian' has become a term of disdain.

The twentieth century has provided many examples of people who, through their own charismatic personalities, have triumphed against great odds - such as Winston Churchill, Martin Luther King, Nelson Mandela and Mahatma Ghandi. Their 'great man' leadership emerged at a time in which it was desperately needed – making it very hard to replicate though of course wider lessons may be learned from study of their lives.

Alimo-Metcalfe (1995) and Goffee and Jones (2000) argue that the modern study of leadership began with Trait theory in the 1920's which stated that people are born with certain characteristics or traits, some of which are associated with effective and proficient leadership (Stodgill, 1974). The various traits researched included physical, personality and social characteristics along with personal abilities and skills (House and Podsakoff, 1994). Trait theories were largely designed to try to predict whether an individual would manifest leadership ability. It was argued that having a leader with these traits was crucial to the success of an organisation. However, later reviews (Stodgill, 1948) reported the lack of any consistent relationship between individual traits and leadership and this encouraged researchers to explore alternative leadership paradigms. The British Army moved away from the use for officer selection of Trait Theory (assumed to be a function of social class) towards a more psychologically based leadership assessment approach during World War 2. This new War Office Selection Board shaped the modern assessment centre (based on leadership competences and potential rather than traits) now common across much of Western business.

Higgs (2003) argued that adopting a sense-making approach to the development of an effective leadership paradigm provides us with two very clear patterns of leadership. The first is that the personality of the leader is a determinant of their effectiveness (Hogan and Hogan, 2001; Collins, 2001b). The second pattern suggests that effective leaders are differentiated from other leaders through the exercise of a relatively small range of skills or competencies (Kouzes and Posner, 1998; Goffee and Jones, 2000; Higgs and Rowland, 2001; Hogan and Hogan, 2001). The choice of how these skills and competencies are exercised is determined by the personality of the individual leader. Higgs (2003) summarises this synergy between personal characteristics and exercise of skills.

Personal characteristics:
- *Authenticity* – being genuine and not 'playing a role' to manipulate
- *Integrity* – being consistent in what you say and do
- *Will* – a drive to lead, and persistence in working towards a goal.
- *Self-belief* – realistic evaluation of capabilities and belief you can achieve
- *Self-awareness* –understanding of 'who you are', how you feel and how others see you

Skills areas:
- *Envision* – identify a future picture, which helps people direct effort
- *Engage* – helping people understand the vision and how to contribute.
- *Enable* –belief in the potential of individuals, and creating the environment in which these can be released
- *Inquire* – being open to real dialogue
- *Develop* – working with people to build capability

'Researchers, in their quest to theoretically explain the emergence of leadership, have moved beyond the trait approach and attempted to provide sound justifications for its presence. These justifications appear to be similar to the general outlook and understanding of leadership which prevailed in the early years of the (Muslim) state', (Ali, A. in Metcalfe and Mimouni, 2011).

The Traits approach does not however 'provide us with a definitive list of which traits make leaders and there is no consideration of the relationship with leadership outcomes' (Schedlitzki and Edwards, 2014).

Leadership Styles theory

'When travelling on a journey, even if there are only three of you, make one a leader'

(Prophet Muhammad, reported by Abu Sa'id Al-Khudri and Abu Hurairah in Book 8, Hadith 5)

Work on understanding the impact of leadership styles largely centered on two paradigms – 'people versus task' or 'directive versus participative' styles (Schedlitzki and Edwards, 2014). Adair (1973) brought together into a new model the three elements of task, team and individual which he called Action Centred Leadership. Adair developed this group model to address the inadequacies of trait theories, while encompassing and endorsing much of the thinking by Maslow and Herzberg about human needs and motivation. The model was developed from observations of leaders and their followers. Adair visualised his theory in a diagram of three overlapping circles.

Figure: Adair's Action Centred Leadership

Source of image https://www.oreilly.com/library/view/john-adairs-100/9780857081780/08_part01.html

The overlapping illustrates that each function is interdependent. If one element is missing or weak then the other elements will suffer. Adair said that leaders should concentrate on:

- Task Completion (achieve the task)
- Creating and sustaining a group of people that work together as a team (build and sustain a team) and
- Development of individuals within the team (develop the individual).

These three objectives can be achieved through actions referred to as leadership functions. He proposed that goals and objectives were SMART (Specific, Measurable, Achievable, Realistic and Time-Constrained). A leader should evaluate events including an evaluation of performance, training for individuals and identifying lessons from previous experience - in other words a leader should employ reflection as a conscious development tool. Adair argued leadership functions included maintaining overall control of a project, implementation of control systems and self-control. A leader needs to delegate tasks effectively and monitor the team's skills to increase efficiency and 'value for money'. Adair believed an excellent leader achieved maximum results with the use of minimum resources and recommended leading by example in order to build credibility and influence. If a team does not feel their leader believes in their objectives then it will lose motivation and focus. Adair believed that leadership can be taught and that a person can become a successful leader through effectively applying his action-centred leadership model. Adair was one of the first proponents of leadership development. It has been said that 'leadership is the art of creating the belief that an intense personal relationship exists between the team as a whole, the individuals and the leader so that the task is completed.'

In an influential HBR article Goleman (2000) explored which leadership style is the most effective. Research has shown that there are six key styles used by leaders and some are more effective than others.

The styles shown to have **a negative** impact on teams and organisations are
- Coercive ('do what I tell you')
- Pacesetting ('do as I do, now').

The styles shown to have **a positive** impact on teams and organisations are
- Authoritative ('come with me')
- Coaching ('what else?')
- Democratic ('what do you think?')
- Affiliative ('people come first')

Interestingly, the research showed that the style with the greatest positive impact is Authoritative but the most effective overall approach was for a leader to master several of these positive styles and to be able to switch between them.

Skills of leadership and management

In the second half of the twentieth century numerous leadership studies (Schedlitzki and Edwards, 2014) proposed that the skill set of managers and leaders comprised three distinct parts - conceptual (at the top of organisations), human (in the middle) and technical (at the bottom of organisations). This started to inform deeper thinking about the competences of leadership and the systems approaches to leadership theory. Mintzberg (1975) researched what managers actually do in their day to day activities and classified them into interpersonal, informational and decision-making activities. Mintzberg has been criticised by McCall and Sergist (1980) who suggest that the roles lack specificity and that a number of items under each role are related not to a single factor but to several factors.

Intelligences of leadership

Traditional understanding of intelligence has been narrowly focused on IQ tests but increasingly there is acceptance within leadership studies that leadership requires more than this including emotional, spiritual and moral intelligences (Gill, 2006). These may alternatively be described as wisdoms.

Emotional intelligence in leadership

There is a growth of literature relating to the emotional aspects of organisational life (Fineman, 1997) and the challenges to the dominance of analytical and rational leadership paradigms (Goffee and Jones, 2001; Higgs and Dulewicz, 2002). A significant component of this literature is the rapid growth in research into emotional intelligence. Emotional intelligence has been defined as the capacity to understand our emotions and manage them effectively, and to understand and effectively manage the emotions of others (Goleman 1995, Mayer and Salovey, 1997). Over the past two decades, emotional intelligence has emerged as an aspect of effective leadership, with evidence suggesting that emotional competencies rather than intellectual capabilities are the differentiating factors in job performance and leadership success (Goleman 1995, 1998, Goleman et al., 2002). Although not the first leadership thinker to articulate the significance of emotional intelligence, Goleman helped connect the concept to competency research and assessment. He introduced a theoretical model of emotional intelligence that evolved to include 18 competencies arranged in four clusters: self-awareness (understanding yourself), self-management (managing yourself), social awareness (understanding others), and relationship management (managing others).

'An emotional competency is a learned capability based on emotional intelligence that results in outstanding performance at work'

(Goleman, 1998)

Goleman asserted that while emotional intelligence is more important for all jobs than both IQ and technical skills, it is significantly more important for leadership roles. Indeed he said that the higher one progresses in an organisation the more important emotional intelligence becomes. Some support for this view was provided by Dulewicz (1999) who reported an analysis of competencies seen as important by a sample of UK company directors. Further support was subsequently provided in a study by Higgs and Dulewicz (2000), in which the differences between the emotional intelligence competencies of chairmen/CEO's, executive directors and managers were examined

Emotional intelligence has been positively correlated with overall job performance (Dulewicz et al., 2005) and the classroom performance of professionals (Sue-Chan and Latham, 2004). Another study found a predictive relationship between emotional intelligence and transformational leadership (Mandell and Pherwani, 2003). The influence of emotional intelligence on team performance has also been found to be considerable (Druskat and Wolff, 2001; Jordan and Troth, 2004; Lopes et al., 2005). The existence of different kinds of intelligence beyond IQ has a solid theoretical and empirical foundation (Gardner, 1993, Salovey and Mayer, 1990). The competency-based model of emotional intelligence proposed by Goleman (2001) has been designed specifically for workplace applications. The competencies underlie four general abilities:

1. *Self-awareness* – the ability to understand feelings and accurate self-assessment.
2. *Self-management* – the ability to manage internal states, impulses and resources.
3. *Social awareness* – the ability to read people and groups accurately.
4. *Relationship management* – the ability to induce desirable responses in others.

Goleman proposes that the emotional competencies are job skills that can be learned. Within this context, Goleman defines emotional intelligence as the ability to recognise and regulate emotions both within the self and others. Brown and Dzendrowskyj (2018) explain how our brains are hard wired to make sense of what is happening around us and that this is done fastest at the emotional level which we then rationalise in our frontal lobes. They write 'an understanding of the emotional system is a critical part of a leader's armamentarium of leadership skills – not only to be attuned to every signal that is coming in but also because the leader's emotional system informs the systems of all those that are being led. For their brains it is serious data too'.

Spiritual intelligence in leadership

Zohar and Marshall (2001) describe this as 'the intelligence with which we address and solve problems of meaning and value'. This is a comparatively under-developed area in Western leadership literature and practice, which may reflect the increasing secularisation of Western societies. However, this is not the case in Islamic settings where a more integrative approach to life and leadership is the cultural norm. There is much spiritual wisdom for leadership to be shared and rediscovered from East to West and South to North. And there is much wisdom within Judeo-Christian traditions which needs to be reconnected to mainstream leadership research and thinking.

'When God wants to punish the sheep, He sends them a blind shepherd'

(Hebrew Proverb in Adair, 2018)

Greenleaf (1977) proposed a theory of Servant Leadership in which leaders emerge through their desire or ability to serve the needs of others. The servant leader views their leadership role as a gift to others - a sacred trust - and believes that the servant leader grows other leaders. Greenleaf advises that the test of a true servant leader is whether those served 'become healthier, wiser, freer, more autonomous, more likely to help themselves to become (servant leaders)'. Servant leadership is based on a motivation to meet the needs of others – not doing their job for them but enabling them to do their job more effectively for themselves. Servant leadership is values-based. Interestingly, the motto of the UK's Royal Military Academy Sandhurst is 'serve to lead'.

'Leadership is not about being in charge. Leadership is about taking care of those in your charge'

(Simon Sinek, 2019)

Moral intelligence in leadership

Moral intelligence is 'the ability to differentiate right from wrong according to universal moral principles', (Schedlitzki and Edwards, 2014). For the Islamic leader seeking to walk in the right path this should be second nature as they live and practice Islamic values. One of the struggles for contemporary leaders is to live a life of integrity, honesty and truthfulness. Many of the troubles of organisations can be traced back to leadership decisions which have been made without a moral compass. We live in times in which spiritual and moral intelligence is needed more than ever. For some this is expressed through faith and for others it is through an ethical framework.

◈ THEME 3: The study of Contingency and Leader-Member Exchange (LMX) theories

Behavioural and Situational Theories

The limitations of Trait theory were responded to by researching the behaviours and style of leaders (Alimo-Metcalfe, 1995). An example of this approach is provided by the Blake and Mouton model (1964) who believed that there was a 'best' style. Leadership experience, however, provided examples of apparent success employing 'less desirable' styles (Higgs and Rowland, 2001). The limitations of style theories were the catalyst for the application of contingency theory to leadership. An example is that developed by Hershey and Blanchard (1969, 1993) who maintained that it was not the leader's style which led to effectiveness, but rather the ability of the leader to adapt their style to the changing needs of their followers (the 'situation'). This may vary between levels of Directing, Coaching, Supporting or Delegating.

Despite the fact that behavioural approaches were not able to determine a 'one best leadership style', they did further the study of leadership, determining that behaviour was a factor which explained leadership effectiveness within a given context or setting.

The behavioural approaches toward leadership gave rise to situational analyses of leadership that were popular from the late 1960s to late 1970s. Situational approaches focused on the effect that certain variables would have on the relationship between leader traits and behaviors and outcomes.

Leader- Member Exchange (LMX)

LMX theory moved the focus of leadership research 'onto the individual follower and the dyadic relationship between leader and follower. This was in stark contrast to the traits, styles and contingency approaches to leadership that treated followers as passive recipients of leadership as exerted by the leader' (Schedlitzki and Edwards, 2014). Researchers introduced the concept of in-group and out-group behaviours. In-group relationships are rich and individually negotiated; out-group relationships are more formalised and contractualised. LMX theories went on to encourage leaders to build large numbers of high quality exchanges leading to mature partnerships with a small number of trusted subordinates. LMX has some conceptual limitations particularly in how such dyadic relationships develop over time and how relationships impact work groups.

∽❧ THEME 4: **study of Charismatic and Transformational leadership**

Charismatic leadership

Charismatic leadership tends to emerge in times of crisis or great need. A charismatic leader will typically have a strong end engaging personality along with a compelling or radical vision for the future which attracts followers (Yukl, 2010). Davis and Gardner (2012) suggest that there is some consensus on the conditions which facilitate the rise of a charismatic leader which include the leader who has extraordinary gifts; a crisis; a revolutionary or radical solution; followers willing to invest their belief in the leader; and validation of the leader through their repeated successes (in Schedlitzki and Edwards, 2014). Some writers suggest there are many types of charismatic leadership including heroic, paternalistic, missionary and majestic. One inherent danger with charismatic leadership is that followers may attach to such a leader in an unhealthy way where the leader 'demands complete loyalty to him personally, right or wrong' (Adair, 2018). Gill (2006) further suggests that 'charismatic leadership appears to be dysfunctional in predictable conditions, perhaps because it may generate unnecessary change'.

Transactional Leadership

Whereas classical leaders did not think too much about their followers, the transactional leader is aware that followers have needs, skills and potential. Transactional leaders will negotiate with followers in order to achieve goals. The 'contract' between leader and follower is based on contingent rewards, setting expectations and goals in return for reward and recognition.

> 'The relations of most leaders and followers are transactional—leaders approach followers with an eye to exchanging one thing for another: jobs for votes, or subsidies for campaign contributions. Such [instrumental] transactions comprise the bulk of the relationships'

> *(Burns, 1978)*

Transactional leadership assumes that the follower behaves in the way stipulated by the leader and he will receive the appropriate reward. By contrast, failure to deliver will invoke punishment. The transactional leader generally manages to satisfy the self-interest of the follower. The transactional leader is preoccupied with power and reward and will tend to focus on tactical, short-term issues. More enlightened transactional leaders will have good interpersonal skills and show concern for the welfare of followers. Their skill lies in the ability to gain the cooperation of followers. Transactional leaders will seek to 'barter' with their followers in a manner that is mutually beneficial as long as the benefits do not outweigh the costs. The transactional leader is pragmatic and builds on the need to get the job done. However, in periods of rapid change, the effectiveness of the transactional leader becomes limited, they are unable to generate the additional commitment needed in followers and innovation becomes stuck.

Transformational Leadership

The concept of vision entered the leadership lexicon in the 1980s, when competition was forcing organisations to adapt more speedily to market and technological changes and the need for a credible future became pressing. Organisations were forced to make significant changes to structure (often downsizing) which struck at the heart of long-term psychological contracts with employees about personal job security. Leaders faced the challenge of rapid adaptation but also the need to maintain employee motivation at a time of intense change. To help them survive and prosper, leaders developed and communicated their vision of a realistic, credible and attractive future. In essence, an organisational vision needs to give a sense of uniqueness, set a path or direction of travel and encapsulate a set of values or ideals. While it is true that it is the leader's responsibility to shape and communicate the vision, rarely if ever do they create this on their own. Several groups will play a part in influencing the vision which will take time to come together. The well-articulated vision provides meaning for employees at all levels in the organisation, meaning which is not necessarily provided by strategic or business plans.

Burns (1978) identified that some leaders engage followers not only to make significant achievements but also to encourage them to become leaders in their own right. Burns drew a distinction between transactional and transformational forms of leadership. Put simply, transformational leaders demonstrate a greater concern with the collective interests of the group or organisation than with their own interests. Burns proposed that leader and follower have something to offer each other i.e. a purpose or mission that transcends personal concerns and so begins to address the higher order needs of followers.

> *"The result of transforming leadership is a relationship of mutual stimulation and elevation that converts followers into leaders and may convert leaders into moral agents"*
>
> *(Burns, 1978)*

Bass took Burns' idea of the transformational leader further. Bass (1990) argued that the transactional and transformational were quite separate aspects of leadership and therefore could be employed by a single individual, and that, in fact, many transformational leaders also used a transactional approach. The Bass/ Avolio (1990, 1995) model cites behavioural aspects of the transformational leader known as the Four I's.

- **Idealized Influence** (closely related to Charisma): as expressed through the leader's behaviour of creating and communicating a vision and by the followers' reactions, such as trust. Followers are likely to develop a strong emotional attachment with such a leader. Charisma on its own was insufficient to create transformation. Charisma can be 'good' (*socialised*) in that the leader cares about the needs of their followers, or 'bad' (*personalised*) in that there is no higher purpose in their mindset, simply the achievement of their objective.

- **Inspirational Motivation.** The ability to inspire: transformational leaders have to be exceptional communicators both in what they say and how they convey it. Effective use will be made of symbols and complex situations are made simple.

- **Individualized Consideration:** such leaders provide encouragement and support, and show trust in and respect for followers as individuals, creating opportunities for further development and building self-confidence. Followers become empowered to seek opportunities for self-development. To achieve this, the leader needs to get to know followers' needs, capabilities and expectations. The leader needs to 'grow' followers' potential.

- The ability to provide **Intellectual Stimulation:** the leader makes followers aware of new ideas and perspectives and challenges them to move beyond habitual forms of behaviour. In so doing, the transformational leader creates a readiness and adaptability to change.

Avery (2004) cites the transformational leader as one capable of capturing hearts and minds using the image of the future communicated to followers. Successful visionary leaders will have a clear vision of the future and also a road map of how to get there. It is imperative that followers share the vision, have contributed to its shaping and are willing to participate in its implementation. The follower interprets the vision into practical ways of working and in being committed to its success. Characteristics of the transformational leader include trustworthiness, honesty, charisma, problem-solving, possessing foresight and decisiveness. Other less positive characteristics may include ruthlessness, being dictatorial and irritable.

Followers will change as they come to believe in the leader's cause. They change because the leader creates a compelling picture of a future, one that is more appealing and exciting than the present, in which they can play a significant part. Ultimately, followers identify with the leader's vision which becomes a motivational driver as they strive to achieve what the leader has communicated. The transformational style generates high levels of engagement and touches the values of followers in a way, it is claimed, that produces better results and more leaders from within an organisation. However, the transformational leader can sometimes develop followers who have unrealistic expectations or an unhealthy psychological dependency on the leader. Such leaders constantly look for and expect unity of purpose; those who do not fit will be made to leave. It can be argued that this form of leadership limits diversity, by discouraging feedback or wider exploration of the vision.

A PhD thesis suggests that transformational leadership models in Iraq and other developing countries have a part to play in building the higher education sector:

'The findings indicate that, regardless of whether we are looking at a western or an eastern context, transformational leadership plays a significant role in promoting a knowledge sharing culture and enhancing both product and process innovation in both private and public HEIs in Iraq'.

(Al-husseini, 2014)

It is clear that transformational leadership can have benefits in multiple cultures.

Authenticity in leadership

Goffee and Jones (2000) and Collins (2001) argue that leadership can be observed as being:

- **Situational:** effective leaders are able to sense the context in which they work and then to beneficially reframe that context. In other words, the context fixes what is required of the leader. In reframing the context, the leader provides a valuable service by repositioning the organisation and its future.

- **Non-hierarchical:** they argue that leadership is not equivalent to having a senior position in an organisation. 'Great organisations have leaders at all levels' Goffee and Jones (2000)

- **Relational:** leaders need followers and followers need a sense of excitement and personal satisfaction.

Their research also shows that, above all other factors, followers want their leaders to be authentic. Leaders' behaviour influences those around them. So it follows that the more authentic a leader is the more 'permission' is given to followers to be likewise. Authenticity can be described as 'trustworthy', 'genuine', and 'free from hypocrisy'. Goffee and Jones explore what behaviours lie at the root of authentic leadership and identify:

- **Consistency between words and deeds:** they practice what they preach.

- **Coherence in role performance:** leaders are capable of 'communicating a consistent underlying thread'. They are capable of showing their real selves and have the confidence to do so.

- **Comfort with themselves:** leaders have the self-confidence to be who they are in the role and, where appropriate, to disclose enough of themselves to allow followers to reaffirm their authenticity. This implies that the leader is able to admit that they don't have all the answers.

Authenticity in leadership is increasingly valued in many societies, yet we have examples in political and commercial life where words and deeds do not match. The natural reaction to such a breach of trust is disappointment, scepticism and cynicism about an individual's trustworthiness. So within organisations if leaders are not authentic, followers' commitment will be curtailed. Conversely the prize is significant for the organisation whose leaders act with authenticity and integrity. It is said that leaders set the tone, or climate, of an organisation. By being authentic, the leader creates an authentic organisational climate. Collins (2001) introduced the concept of Level 5 leadership – characterised by leaders who demonstrate strong 'Professional Will' combined with personal humility. This combination allows them to achieve extraordinary results through the extraordinary relationships they build. They are ambitious for the organisation, drive for results, accept responsibility for failure and share praise for success. The organisations they build are durable and healthy places to work.

❧ THEME 5: leadership models in the Middle East

Ali (in Metcalfe and Mimouni, 2011) writes that the current Middle East bears little resemblance to the eras of the birth of Islam or its 'golden age'. He states that it is more like the 'fragmentation and powerlessness that followed the collapse of Baghdad at the hands of the invading Mongol forces in 1258 CE.' Ali believes in the potential of the region to reinvent itself and that leadership will play a pivotal role in creating healthy organisations and businesses across the region which will become great places to work. This pattern of leadership can flow outwards to positively impact political leadership. The years of political and economic instability across the region do not have to continue. It will however need different models of leadership.

It is fascinating as a Westerner to read the early Islamic paradigms of leadership. It would seem that they contain much leadership wisdom to treasure and which can be adapted to modern challenges. Indeed some writers have argued that early Islamic traditions laid a base for democratic forms of government particularly with Islam's emphasis on consultation and the welfare of the community. I do not want to pretend, however, that the democratic model is working well everywhere. Indeed, in the U.K. it is clear after more than four years of Brexit turmoil that our political system is stretched to breaking point and needs renewal. In the USA the so-called 'disruptive' effects of President Trump and his brand of politics seem to have increased political polarisation. Populism has been used by some racists and extremists across the Western world to make much social and political discourse highly toxic.

> *'Many forms of Government have been tried, and will be tried in this world of sin and woe. No one pretends that democracy is perfect or all-wise. Indeed it has been said that democracy is the worst form of Government except for all those other forms that have been tried from time to time....'*

> *(Speech by Winston Churchill, 11 November 1947)*

The emerging consensus across the body of research on managerial leadership in the Middle East region is that Arab leaders are mostly consultative and participative, with some countries favouring benevolent autocratic styles. In the Gulf countries leadership traits which are highly prized include charismatic, values-based, self-protective and considerate dimensions. An Arab proverb says 'It is the tribe that tells the chief how to do the job'. Arabs 'long for a prophetic leader and desire qualities that encompass participation, openness and transparency' (Ali, A. in Metcalfe and Mimouni, 2011). Ali goes on 'most of the empirical findings, conceptual studies and commentaries, in the context of leadership in Islam, assert two things: that leaders are assumed to be consultative and participative and that these leaders promote competency and performance'.

Faris and Abdalla, (2018) write:

'Leadership is based on trust and responsibility, which is subject to accountability in this life and the next. When one of the companions (followers) of the Prophet Muhammad asked for a leadership position, the response he received was insightful and truthful, "You are weak," said the Prophet, "and leadership is a trust; it is a disgrace and regret on the Day of Judgment except for those who claim it rightfully, and fulfill its responsibility." That is the reason that Islam sees leadership as a responsibility and not a privilege. A leader, political or otherwise, has the duty to serve (servant leadership), and his authority is sanctioned by his followers. In Islam, leadership is based on merit and competence, it is not inherited'.

Tabrizi (2018) in a PhD dissertation writes 'Islamic leadership has a much stronger spiritual and religious dimension to it. This can be seen in how Islamic leadership is characterized by religious and spiritual behaviour (i.e., following Qur'anic law); emphasizes motivation from a spiritual sources (e.g., the Qur'an, prayer, etc.); and is oriented towards people and not products (Ankerberg & Burroughs, 2008; Al-Buraey, 1985). The human orientation can be seen as a combination of transformational leadership, servant leadership, and participatory leadership approaches (Mohammad et al., 2015).'

Other researchers have highlighted contradictions in some Middle Eastern countries between espoused leadership models and actual practice. These contradictions are a form of 'mental cheating' (Child, 1976) and Ali (ibid) writes 'Leaders' behaviour... seeks to disguise their authoritarian propensities by projecting a false image of idealism onto their subordinates and followers'.

'Perhaps these contradictions may be responsible, in large part, for current economic and political stagnation and, con-

sequently, for impairing organizational and national performance......The apparent contradictions between the desire for inclusion and consultation and participative approaches and the authoritarian practices hold a key to understanding the current tension between followers and leaders and between governments and their own citizens, and to a large extent to understanding the nature of instability in the region and its accompanying semi-chronic crisis of identity that people in the region experience'

(Ali, A. in Metcalfe and Mimouni, 2011).

We can only hope that leadership will find its 'true path' to generate renewal of teams, organisations, ideas and indeed nations.

∾❧ THEME 6: **An integrative model of leadership – High Performance Teams**
A 21st century model of leadership practice should encourage a contextualised approach which can generate high performance through a combination of approaches drawing from theory in leadership competences, leader-follower relationships, transformational and distributed leadership. These include:

- Emotional intelligence – being able to give and receive feedback
- Sense-making in a changing environment
- Shared Values including appropriate spiritual intelligence
- Collaboration
- Team dynamics
- Flexible use of Authoritative, Affiliative, Coaching and Democratic leadership styles
- Results focus
- Reflective practice
- Commitment to professional standards

Chapters 7 and 8 explore in detail the routes to building and maintaining such high performance. They review global research and practice about High Performance Teams and set out a model to enable high performance to emerge which is both replicable and cross-cultural. This is the first time this leadership literature on high performance has been published in book form.

❧ THEME 7: The future of leadership

What might leadership look like in the future? Avery (2004) argues that leadership may develop away from the notion of a single top leader. Networked organisations, without physical boundaries, will not necessarily need a single leader. Avery speculates that leadership will arise in multiple forms within a single organisation; adaptive, multi-talented and problem-solving. Organisations will be structured into cross functional groups, each self-managing and optimising. Such organisations will be based on reciprocal actions rather than on positional power. No single right answer will be sought rather a sense-making approach will be developed. These new organisational forms will engage in partnerships drawing in customers, contractors, suppliers and competitors. Avery's organic leadership model represents a radical way of thinking about leadership. Control and hierarchy are rejected in favour of trust, continuous change, mutual respect, self-control and self-organisation. Trust is a key here.

'One of the most important lessons we can learn from an examination of economic life is that a nation's well-being, as well as its ability to compete, is conditioned by a single, persuasive cultural characteristic; the level of trust in society'

(Fukuyama cited in Seldon, 2009)

Seldon identified ten features of high trust organisations and countries:
1. Grounded in ethical values
2. Pride and a sense of ownership
3. Wider focus than just profit or personal gain
4. A sense of responsibility rather than rights
5. Regimes which guarantee freedom from fear
6. Wisely led
7. Honest communication
8. People are looked after
9. Family is respected
10. Individuals feel valued

These features resonate strongly with the high performance leadership model I share later in this book. They also resonate strongly with much Islamic leadership practice.

There is an established body of knowledge about leadership which has been developed over the last one hundred years by both academics and practitioners. It is contributing to a growing understanding that leadership and management are co-dependent, contextual and relational. Good leadership is vital for the success of our organisations and economies. This body of knowledge of leadership theory has however been dominated by Western thinking and research and an emerging dialogue is seeking to re-discover leadership wisdom in non-Western traditions (Turnbull et al, 2012). Adair (2010) has written about the leadership of the prophet Muhammad. Beekun and Badawi (1999) have developed further perspectives on Islamic leadership. There is a growing awareness amongst leadership development professionals and thinkers of the place in leadership of 'spiritual intelligence'. These texts contribute to that wider debate on the nature of leadership wisdom.

Leadership needs to be shaped by strong values and practiced by people who have humility and authenticity. The world and the workforce are changing fast and leaders and leadership needs to evolve. Many of the practices of today's leaders were forged in the early 20th century and are no longer fit for purpose. Today's generation demands greater democracy. They want autonomy, the opportunity to develop mastery and make connection with a meaningful purpose (Pink, 2010). This is key work for today's leaders.

❧ Key Wisdom in this chapter

The search for leadership wisdom is rooted in ancient civilisations and continues today

- 'The study of history has been the study of leaders' (Bass, 1990b)
- There are Eastern, Western and Tribal voices of leadership wisdom
- Leadership studies as an academic discipline is a relatively modern phenomenon
- Leadership and management are 'two horses pulling the same cart' (Birkinshaw, 2010)
- Paradigms have been used to try to understand leadership and management (including scientific, psychological and social constructs)
- Leadership theory also focused on individual competences including Traits (now largely discredited), skills, styles and intelligences.
- Key and enduring developments in leadership thinking have been Action Centred Leadership and Goleman's emotional intelligence work on the four positive leadership styles - Authoritative, Coaching, Democratic and Affiliative.
- Spiritual and moral intelligences are increasingly recognised as important
- Situational leadership focuses on the adaptations needed for context
- Transformational leadership is evidenced as a force for change in both Western and Middle Eastern settings

- High Performance Teams represent an integrative model for 21st century leadership in organisations, which resonates with Islamic leadership values

CHAPTER 6

Leadership wisdom in the life of three prophets

In the Qur'an the reader is encouraged to consider prophets as role models to study and learn from.

'Those were the people God guided, follow the guidance they received'

(Qur'an 6:90)

We can acquire wisdom for leadership by studying the lives of the prophets. I will look at three great prophets who are each revered in the Jewish, Christian and Islamic faiths and I will draw out some wisdom for leaders from the examples of their lives.

❧ Prophet Joseph (Yusuf)

Joseph was the young son of Jacob but, due to his father's unwise decision to make him his favourite son, Joseph's siblings grew to hate him. They conspired to fake his death and threw Joseph into a well from where he was later taken by a caravan of merchants. Joseph's wicked brothers returned home and they then lied to Jacob about their evil deed. It must have been hard for Joseph to understand how his life had turned for the worse. Joseph was taken to Egypt where he became a house slave to the chief minister of Egypt, who saw how God blessed Joseph in his work. Joseph's new master trusted him completely.

'And when he (Joseph) attained his full manhood, We gave him power and knowledge: thus do We reward those who do right'

(Qur'an 12:22)

However, in time his master's wife Zulaikha tried to seduce Joseph, who ran from the house rather than succumb to her advances. Joseph, falsely accused, is sent to prison even though his master knows him to be innocent but God blesses Joseph in prison with spiritual wisdom and insight and he becomes able to interpret dreams – which he does correctly for two fellow prisoners from Pharaoh's household. He predicts that the cup bearer will be returned to Pharaoh's court and his position restored and he predicts that the other prisoner (the cook) is executed. The predictions are fulfilled and Joseph hopes he will be remembered by the elevated prisoner and quickly released. However, he was forgotten. Joseph had to continue in prison for a few more years.

This period of Joseph's life was a time of preparation for national leadership but Joseph could not have known how God was using these difficult circumstances to work on his character to develop deeper dependence on God and greater faith. As an adolescent Joseph had been impetuous but over the years Joseph matured under affliction, false accusations and many hardships. God had a greater intention for him but Joseph needed to be prepared by God to take up the huge role planned for him.

In time the released servant remembered Joseph and told Pharaoh about him, explaining that Joseph was an interpreter of dreams and that he was the right man for Pharaoh to listen to about a troubling dream Pharaoh had. Joseph was called from prison and stood before Pharaoh. God gave him wisdom to interpret correctly Pharaoh's dream about a forthcoming famine. Joseph proposed a plan to prepare for the famine and Pharaoh made Joseph controller of the granaries. Ibn Kathir (2019) writes 'Joseph did not mean to seize an opportunity or personal gain…. it was sheer nobleness on his part in that he wanted to ensure that many people would not die as a result'. Joseph took a national leadership position to save the people from starvation, storing corn wisely in the seven years of plenty. It is an extraordinary story of wise leadership which saved the whole nation and also neighbouring countries. Joseph had demonstrated integrity in his personal choice not to commit adultery with his master's wife; learnt patience in prison; held on to his faith despite frequent disappointments and was in time brought before Pharaoh to be honoured and promoted.

After perhaps another ten years Joseph receives a visit from some of his brothers who have travelled from famine-struck Canaan to Egypt in search of corn supplies. They do not recognise Joseph but he recognises them. It would have been understandable if Joseph had decided to take revenge on his brothers but he chose another path. He undertakes an elaborate series of tests to see if his brothers have changed and now regret their decision to sell Joseph as a slave. He manages to conceal his true identity and ascertains that his siblings are indeed full of remorse for their wickedness. Joseph eventually reveals himself after some months of testing his brothers. Joseph forgave his brothers and showed them kindness and love. He had learned the right path. His father Jacob was brought down to Egypt and lived with Joseph until his death. Joseph now understands that God was in all these difficult times of his life and says:

'He was indeed good to me when He took me out of prison and brought you (all here) out of the desert, (even) after Satan had sown enmity between me and my brothers. Verily, my Lord understandeth best the mysteries of all that He planneth to do. For verily, He is full of knowledge and wisdom'

(Qur'an 12: 100)

Joseph's siblings thought that once Jacob had died that Joseph would take revenge on them - they did not believe that Joseph had truly forgiven them. However Joseph, once again misunderstood by his brothers, stood his ground and said:

'Don't be afraid! Am I in the place of God? You intended to harm me, but God intended it for good to accomplish what is now being done, the saving of many lives"

(Genesis 50: 19-20, NIV)

We can be inspired with 'a feeling for the depth of Allah's power and supremacy and the execution of His rulings despite the challenge of human intervention' (Ibn Kathir, 2019). As a leader Joseph was visionary in terms of his plan for salvation from famine – this was transformational leadership. Joseph had learned that God was directing him even through the bad things that happened to him. When others intended to harm him he came to understand that God could turn those evil intentions into good. This was spiritual wisdom. Joseph exercised forgiveness towards his brothers and had also learned the power of not holding on to grudges however justified. Joseph rose above personal considerations and made his decisions as a leader in the best interests of family and community. He is a compelling leadership example for us.

The key leadership wisdom we can apply today from Joseph's story includes the understanding that:
- Difficulties and hardships can be part of God's training for us as leaders
- Personal integrity is a key part of leadership
- Our leadership position should never be used as an op-

portunity for personal gain but rather for the benefit of the wider community

- People may intend to harm you, but God can turn this for good

❧ Prophet Moses (Musa)

Moses is one of the great leaders in the Qur'an, honoured also in Judeo-Christian traditions in the Bible. As a baby his life was threatened by an Egyptian Pharaoh who did not know what great things Joseph had done for Egypt many years before (Exodus 1:8, NIV). This new Pharaoh felt threatened by the growing numbers of Israelites. Pharaoh gave instructions for all male Jewish babies to be thrown into the River Nile at birth but baby Moses was hidden by his parents for three months and then put into a basket of reeds and placed in the tall grass at the river's edge. Baby Moses was found by Pharaoh's daughter and adopted into her family. Moses was raised in Pharaoh's royal household.

Many years later Moses saw an Egyptian guard beating one of the Israelites and Moses killed the Egyptian and hid the body. Terrified of being found out the next day he fled into the desert. He made friends with Jethro, priest of Midian and later married his daughter. This period of ten years was a time of major preparation during which God 'prepared for His prophet the tools he would need later on to righteously bear the commands of Allah the Exalted', (Ibn Kathir, 2019). Many years later Pharaoh died and was replaced by a new king. At this time, Moses had a spiritual experience in the desert, with God instructing Moses:

'Go thou to Pharaoh, for he has indeed transgressed all bounds'

(Qur'an 20:24)

God commissioned Moses to return to Egypt. Moses was initially reluctant to accept the command but eventually did so with the help of his brother Aaron.

> *'(Moses) said: O my Lord! Expand me my breast; ease my task for me; and remove the impediment from my speech, so they may understand what I say: and give me a Minister from my family, Aaron, my brother; add to my strength through him, and make him share my task: that we may celebrate thy praise without stint, and remember Thee without stint: For Thou art He that (ever) regardeth us. (Allah) said: Granted is thy prayer, O Moses!'*

> *(Qur'an 20: 25- 36)*

Moses can be described as a reluctant leader who did not have great self-confidence. God understood his weaknesses and gave him a trusted helper in his brother Aaron. Unus (2014) writes 'his plea for help represents the hallmark of a great leader, full of humility and dependent on his Lord for success'. Leaders who are unsure of themselves often make the mistake of only recruiting people into their team who are less able than themselves (Unus, 2014) but Moses shows us a better way - to recruit someone who will compensate for a skills gap. Moses perceived himself to be lacking in ability to speak in public and so he asked God to give him someone who could make up for that shortfall. Moses entered the palace of Pharaoh to ask for the Israelite people to be let go but Pharaoh repeatedly refused and then made their work as slaves even harder. There followed a series of ten plagues upon Egypt with the River Nile being turned to blood, plagues of frogs, gnats and flies, dead animals, sores, hailstones, locusts and then darkness. The Israelites were kept free of the plagues by God. Moses showed courage in continually challenging the all-powerful Pharaoh. The final plague brought the death of every firstborn male child in Egypt, during what became known as the Passover Feast. Pharaoh's firstborn son died that night and Moses was summoned to be told the Israelites could now leave with all their possessions. Moses led the people across the Sea of Reeds, experiencing God's miraculous interventions against Pharaoh and his army, who had pursued them in a change of heart. The Egyptian army was utterly destroyed in the sea and the Israelites escaped.

Moses now had the leadership task of taking the people to the Promised Land of Canaan. This might have sounded easier than getting them out of the clutches of a cruel Pharaoh but their journeying in the desert went on for 40 years because God was displeased with the continual complaints of the Israelites most of whom showed no faith in God's ability to protect them. They kept returning to their polytheistic ways and made a false God to worship in the desert. Moses was visited in the desert by his father in law Jethro who saw what God had done for the people and marvelled. But Jethro watched what Moses was doing, deciding all the legal cases from the people from morning until night, and he said to Moses:

> 'You and these people who come to you will only wear yourselves out. The work is too heavy for you: you cannot handle it alone. Listen now to me and I will give you some advice, and may God be with you.... Select capable men from all the people- men who fear God, trustworthy men who hate dishonest gain – and appoint them as officials over thousands, hundreds, fifties and tens. Let them serve as judges for the people at all times, but let them bring every difficult case to you; the simple cases they can decide for themselves. That will make your load lighter, because they will share it with you'

> *(Exodus 18: 18-23, NIV)*

Moses took this sensible advice and made the necessary changes, building a team of wise deputies who could carry the burden with him. This left Moses freer to focus on the leadership tasks which only he could do.

The key leadership wisdom we can learn from the life of Moses is that it is important as a leader to:
- Identify those with leadership potential who are trustworthy and develop their capabilities
- Delegate work to them
- Trust them to get on with that work
- Be humble enough to take advice from wise people

❧ A story of the leadership of Prophet David (Dawud) by Ibn Kathir (1300 – 1373)

'When the two armies faced each other, Goliath challenged any soldier from King Saul's army to single combat, as was the custom of battle in those days. Goliath also wanted to show off his strength. The men were terrorized, and no one had enough courage to volunteer. The king offered the hand of his pretty daughter in marriage to the man who would fight Goliath, but even this tempting offer did not change the deadly silence among his soldiers. Then, to everyone's surprise, a youth stepped forward. A roar of laughter echoed from the enemy's side, and even Saul's men shook their heads. The young man was David (Dawud), from the city of Bethlehem. His elderly father had chosen three of his sons to join Saul's army. He had instructed the youngest one, David, not to take part in the fighting but to help the army in other ways and to report to his father daily on what was happening on the war front.

Although Saul was very impressed by the youth's courage, he said: "I admire your courage, but you are no match for that mighty warrior. Let the strong men come forward." David, however, had already decided and was willing to meet the challenge. Proudly, he told the king that only the day before he had killed a lion which had threatened his father's sheep, and on another occasion he had killed a bear. He asked Saul not to judge him by his appearance, for he feared no man or wild beast. Saul, surprised by young David's brave stance, agreed: "My brave soldier, if you are willing, then may Allah guard you and grant you strength!"

The king dressed David in battle armor and handed him a sword, but David was not used to wearing battle dress. He felt uncomfortable in it, and it obstructed his movements. He removed the armor, then collected a few pebbles and filled his leather pouch with them. He slung it over his shoulder next to his sling. With his wooden staff in hand, he began to walk towards the enemy. Saul was worried and asked him how on earth, with a sling and a couple of stones was he going to defend himself against the giant? David replied: "Allah Who protected me from the claws of the bear and the fangs of the lion will certainly protect me from this brute!"

When Goliath set eyes on the lean young man who looked like a boy, he laughed loudly and roared: "Are you out to play war with one of your playmates, or are you tired of your life? I will simply cut off your head with one swipe of my sword!" David shouted back: "You may have armor, shield, and sword, but I face you in the name of Allah, the Lord of the Israelites, Whose laws you have mocked. Today you will see that it is not the sword that kills but the will and power of Allah!"

So saying, he took his sling and placed in it a pebble from his pouch. He swung and aimed it at Goliath. The pebble shot from the whirling sling with the speed of an arrow and hit Goliath's head with great force. Blood gushed out, and Goliath thumped to the ground, lifeless, before he had a chance to draw his sword. When the rest of his men saw their mighty hero slain, they took to their heels. The Israelites followed in hot pursuit, taking revenge for their years of suffering at the hands of their enemy, killing every soldier they could lay hands on. In this battle the Israelites regained the glory and honor that had been lost for a long time.

David became a hero overnight. Saul kept his word and married his daughter Michal to the young warrior and took him under his wing as one of his chief advisors.

Almighty Allah declared: *'So they routed them by Allah's Leave and David killed Goliath, and Allah gave him (David) the kingdom (after the death of Saul and Samuel) and wisdom, and taught him of that which He willed. And if Allah did not check one set of people by means of another, the earth would indeed be full of mischief. But Allah is full of Bounty to the Alamin (mankind, jinns and all that exist)'. (Ch 2:251Quran)*

David became the most famous man among the Israelites. However, he was not inveigled by this; he was not a prisoner of fame or leadership but a prisoner of Allah's love. Therefore, after killing Goliath he went out into the desert in the company of nature, glorifying Almighty Allah and contemplating His favors. *'Verily, We made the mountains to glorify Our Praises with him (David) in the Ashi (after the mid-day till sunset) and Ishraq (after the sunrise till mid-day). And (so did) the birds assembled: all with him (David) did turn (to Allah, glorified His Praises). We made his kingdom strong and gave him wisdom and sound judgment in speech and decision'. (Ch 38:18-20 Quran)*

One day David found Saul in a worried state. He sensed something strange in Saul's attitude towards him. That night, when he shared his feeling with his wife, she started to weep bitterly and said: "O David, I will never keep any secrets from you." She told him that her father had become jealous of his popularity and feared that he would lose his kingdom to him. She advised him to be on his guard. This information shocked David very much. He prayed and hoped that Saul's good nature would overcome the darker side of his character. The following day, Saul summoned David to inform him that Canaan had gathered its forces and would march on the kingdom. He ordered David to advance on them with the army and not to return unless victory was gained. David sensed that this was an excuse to get rid of him; either the enemy would kill him, or in the thick of battle, Saul's henchmen might stab him in the back. Yet he hastened with his troops to meet the army of Canaan. They fought the Canaanites bravely, without thinking of their own safety. Allah granted them victory, and David lived to return to Saul.

Unfortunately, this only increased Saul's fear, so he plotted to kill David. Such is jealousy that not even a daughter's well-being mattered. Michal learned of her father's plan and hurried to warn her husband. David gathered some food and things, mounted his camel and fled. He found a cave in which he remained hidden for many days. After a time, David's brothers and some citizens joined forces with him. Saul's position became very weak, for he began to rule with a heavy hand. He ill-treated the learned, tortured the reciters of the Talmud, and terrorized his soldiers. This worsened his position, and his subjects began to turn against him. He decided to go to war against David. Hearing this news, David marched to confront Saul's army.

The king's army had travelled a great distance and was overcome by fatigue, so they decided to rest in a valley, where they fell asleep. Quietly, David crept up to the sleeping Saul, removed his spear, and cut off a piece of his garment with the sword. David then awakened the king and told him: "Oh king, you come out seeking me, but I do not hate you, and I do not want to kill you. If I did, I would have killed you when you were asleep. Here is a piece of your garment. I could have hacked your neck instead, but I did not. My mission is that of love, not malice." The king realized his mistake and begged for forgiveness. Time passed and Saul was killed in a battle in which David did not take part. David succeeded Saul, for the people remembered what he had done for them and elected him king. So it was that David the Prophet was also a king. Allah strengthened the dominion of David and made him victorious. His kingdom was strong and great; his enemies feared him without engaging in war with him.

———*———

David divided his working day into four parts: one to earn a living and to rest, one to pray to his Lord, one to listen to the complaints of his people, and the last part to deliver his sermons. He also appointed deputies to listen to his subjects' complaints so that in his absence people's problems might not be neglected.'
(*source: Islam Awareness, 2019*)

What leadership lessons can we draw from the life of David as narrated by Ibn Kathir?

As a young man David developed courage and trust in God as he fought a lion and a bear. He showed the same courage and trust in God as he stepped forward to fight the giant Goliath. He was rewarded by God with a great victory who later gave him 'wisdom and sound judgment in speech and decision' (Qur'an 38:18-20). David was humble and sought God's help in his decision- making 'Verily, he was ever oft-returning in all matters and in repentance toward Allah' (Qur'an 38:17).

David maintained what we today call a work-life balance as a leader, with division of his day into four parts covering earning a living and resting; prayer; listening to the complaints of his people; and delivering his sermons. We also learn that he built his team, appointing 'deputies to listen to his subjects' complaints'. Good leaders delegate to wise people and trust their team to act.

In his leadership David was described as skilful, caring and nurturing. Indeed the book of Psalms pictures him as a shepherd of Israel and says that 'David shepherded them with integrity of heart; with skillful hands he led them' (Psalm 78:72, NIV). David's leadership was a combination of great competence with great humanity.

✖ **The key leadership wisdom in the story of David is that it is important to:**
- Trust in God for the courage we need even when faced with a 'giant' problem
- Admit our mistakes and ask God for forgiveness
- Maintain a work-life balance
- Delegate authority to trusted team members
- View leadership as the work of a skilful, nurturing shepherd

CHAPTER 7

Leadership wisdom to create high performance

❧ PART ONE: **the Journey**

This chapter has been a working lifetime in the writing. It is an output of the learning I made sense of, and reflected upon, during 4 decades of leading people and teams and then working as a leadership development consultant nationally and internationally. Chapters 7 and 8 contain some parts originally written for the unpublished Masters dissertation of this author, Nelson (2005b).

My first leadership experience was as a platoon commander in the British Army. At the world-famous Royal Military Academy, Sandhurst I was introduced to John Adair's 'three circles' model of small group leadership. This focused my attention on three elements of 'achieve the task, build the team and develop individuals'. I found that those simple truths of how to create something special in a group worked very well and I have kept them close throughout my career. They have proved themselves to be wisdom for leadership. I added some police service in London to my career portfolio. The stone rolled on and I found myself working as a postman delivering letters – this time on the receiving end of indifferent leadership. I started to climb the ladder of promotion in what was then the General Post Office – a sleepy organisation which had just emerged from the Civil Service. It was characterised by command and control management - 'do as I say'. Power was vested in position. Change was very slow. Most people did enough work to stay out of trouble but few did more than what was asked.

By the mid 1980's I had been promoted into senior management in what had then become known as Royal Mail. I was responsible for mail deliveries across the whole of West London with thirteen large delivery offices. I experienced the extremes of well managed delivery offices with pride in their work and high quality of service to one in which anarchy reigned and embattled managers were being physically intimidated. My first year in that role was spent simply regaining control in the chaotic delivery office , getting rid of bullies and industrial 'saboteurs' and lifting the confidence of my managers. Then one day something simply remarkable happened. It was simple because it was someone saying a few words to me. It was remarkable because it had never happened in that way before. I had many delivery offices to look after in my area but virtually every day I visited my 'troubled' one. On entering the office I would wish any delivery staff I saw a cheery 'Good morning' but I was always ignored. I was seen as 'a suit' and suits were not to be trusted or acknowledged. I had worked hard over the year to make the office a safe place to work in, with a clear focus on providing good customer service. I ensured people were treated fairly but firmly. My habit of personal courtesy was part of that approach. As I walked across the dimly lit, and slightly unsafe, basement car park I gave my greeting to an older postman walking towards me. He looked me in the eye and replied 'Good morning'. I knew in that moment that things had turned. It was a significant moment. One good heart had been reached and if there was one then there would be more. Mutual respect had been established. I realised that the decent people wanted to see order and purpose return. They were responding to the lines I had drawn in the sand about what was acceptable behaviour. I had used everything I had learned about leadership to that date using command and control management, underpinned by personal integrity, to establish a platform on which we could build better operational performance. And to an extent, it worked.

What I was to learn next meant *unlearning* much of those techniques. By 1988 I was Head of Planning at Royal Mail in Watford. I watched in amazement as my new boss David Legge, District Head Postmaster, engaged in what he called 'catching people doing things right'. I had spent years catching people doing things wrong and correcting them but this was entirely different. He went out of his way to find examples of excellence and celebrated them with words of thanks, public acknowledgement, thank you cards, and occasional tangible rewards. This was his conscious experiment to try something different in his leadership style to see if it worked. The atmosphere was so positive, without compromising on difficult conversations or necessary challenges. Over four years I was part of a Board of management in which every member was dedicated to raising performance through high engagement of the workforce – and we saw our entire key performance indicators rise to the top of national league tables year after year. I realised that it was possible to achieve superior performance without command and control being the dominant dynamic. Indeed, this engaging culture required that command and control be left behind. There was excitement and energy across the workforce. I had touched a very different future.

Following reorganisation I was promoted to be Delivery Area Manager for the Watford, St Albans and Enfield areas. My departing former boss said "You have the hardest task, to take over a high performing operation and keep it there". I wanted to prove him wrong. I decided to take what I had learned from him and amplify it using every opportunity to deepen workforce engagement, build management and leadership capacity and pursue excellence at each turn. Adair's words rang in my ears - achieve the task, build the team and develop individuals. And I would do that this time by catching people do things right.

I had over 1450 people in the enlarged team with 70 managers, serving over 500,000 customers. But as I followed my instincts I saw over the next four years a continuing rise in the metrics whether it was customer service, quality of next day delivery, budget or employee satisfaction. We truly excelled together. I was learning the power of gaining hearts and minds and tapping into the potential of many hundreds of people. Discretionary effort was being increased daily. I was living in a high performance environment, which was going from strength to strength. By 1999 I was heading up a national planning team deploying a balanced scorecard across the whole of Royal Mail's UK operation. I had a team of 14 senior managers charged with training 3000 operational managers across England, Wales, Scotland and N. Ireland in this new approach to accountability for results. I discovered twelve months into that role that what this project was attempting to do was change the culture of the organisation. Personal accountability for results was being resisted. My diagnosis of the roll-out problems told me that I needed to focus on my team - to raise their influencing skills and build them into a high performing unit. I had never attempted to do that with a group physically dispersed over four countries. I found help from a Royal Mail training consultant who devised a programme to help me achieve my objective of raising the influencing skills of my team. The team was forged into a high performing unit and the project successfully completed ahead of time and under budget. I was beginning to understand the transferability of the high performance mix. A leader can create the conditions in which high performance could naturally emerge.

By 2002 I felt uneasy with my working life. I was in my mid 40's and wanted to leave corporate life and set up my own business. I negotiated a severance package and with that money established a training business. I wanted to pass on some of the lessons I had learned to a wider audience. I commenced study on a MBA with a specialism in Leadership Studies at Strathclyde University. That Master's degree swept me into new learning streams. This included experiential learning at the Leadership Trust Foundation near Hereford – a series of intense, experiential learning courses which deeply impacted me. I learnt the power of effective peer feedback and reflection, observing the impact of skilful facilitators who could create a psychologically safe space for a group to accelerate their learning. I decided to focus my MBA experience on high performance. I wanted to study the ideas, concepts, theory and practice I had seen and tried in my work and to look at new ideas, research and thinking. What did high performance mean in Marketing, Operations, Finance, Strategy and so on? In the meantime my training business did not do well. I was not networked enough to run a venture like that and I sought interim management opportunities. I started an assignment with the Learning & Skills Council in central London. This was an opportunity for another experiment, creating a high performing team out of a dysfunctional one. Looking back I can see God's hand leading me from one formative experience to another.

The details of this experiment are in the '*Show Me*' Case Study below. What it allowed me to do was crystallise my practice and thinking about high performance, carrying out some action learning as part of my dissertation. I started to formulate a model of high performance. I undertook a literature search on global practice in high performance. This meta-research ('study of studies') looked for the compelling and enduring themes which underpinned high performance culture. I wanted to cut through the consultant-speak and management jargon to understand what kept surfacing as the common threads. I wanted to develop a model of useful learning about high performance.

I left the LSC in 2006 and re-launched my consultancy business. During this period I had the privilege of taking up an interim role with the Centre for Excellence in Leadership as Director of the Principals Qualifying Programme (PQP). I improved this high profile and very new leadership development programme, which the UK Government had mandated for new Principals of Further Education Colleges in England. I worked with over 150 Principals and Chief Executives in the sector, shaping a programme which incorporated good practice from around the world. Many existing Principals chose to attend even though it was not a requirement for existing Principals. I researched what other countries were doing in developing leadership for their Principals and I established a design framework which matched the very best globally. I introduced my high performance model on the PQP programme team, coaches and assessors and once again it worked. We had stunning results. The Government department which sponsored the programme commissioned an external evaluation and said it was the best impact and evaluation report they had ever read.

Iraqi-born Ali Hadawi, one of the UK Principals on the PQP, had been closely involved with the reconstruction of the Iraqi vocational education sector since 2004. He shared his PQP experiences with colleagues (Deans) in Iraq and in 2009 we were visited by a group of senior policy makers from the Iraqi Ministry of Higher Education. They liked what they saw and in time asked for a tailored version of what would be called the Deans Qualifying Programme. I went back into freelance work in late 2009 and began working with this Iraqi group, first in the UK, then in Turkey and finally in Iraq. Part of their development programme included the high performance model. This model has now been refined in workshops with hundreds of middle managers, senior leaders and Chief Executives in public and private sector organisations throughout N. Ireland, England and Iraq. It has successfully travelled across organisational boundaries and national cultures and is robust in different contexts and settings. It has been used successfully in teams which were already strong and in teams which were dysfunctional.

This chapter shares the accumulated wisdom of many across the world who have struggled to articulate and understand just what it is that leaders do to create and sustain high performance. And you will see that, once it is in place, the leadership task changes and the high performance change agent has to step out of the way to allow high performance to flourish.

The case for a different workplace

We live in a world where celebrity status is desired and admired. Thousands dream of winning a reality or talent show and being catapulted to a celebrity lifestyle in which paparazzi take pictures which are then pored over by magazine readers. Millions more watch TV shows in which celebrities, already established in their own fields, struggle with unfamiliar challenges in the ballroom or jungle. In such a world, it is too easy to translate these values of celebrity to leadership and assume that organisational results can be obtained relatively quickly through the direction of a single individual deemed to have talent. This myth is reinforced by some TV celebrity chefs and businessmen who parade a pacesetting 'leadership' style which is often little more than bullying and intimidation. Great entertainment it may be, but it is deeply damaging to the image of business and the perception of leadership.

'Why should anyone be led by you?' by Rob Goffee & Gareth Jones (2000) is a book which has engaged leaders over the last few years. A parallel question is 'Why do you want to be a leader?' Leaders need to think about their personal motivation for seeking and practising leadership. Do they want to achieve some kind of celebrity status in the workplace or do they want to serve the people they lead, help them grow and create superb results as they do so? This chapter is written for those wanting to understand the nature of such an organic approach to leadership. Organic means to be 'without unnatural additives, fertilisers or pesticides' (Collins Dictionary). An organic approach to leadership is also without unnatural additives – it is true and authentic.

There are many books written on high performance and it can be confusing to know which ones to read and which models to experiment with. Where should you begin to introduce a high performance culture? How do you nurture high performance once it is established? I have researched over two decades what it is that leaders do to create and sustain high performance. I have looked at studies from across the world and identified the consistent practices and approaches which emerged from these books, articles and academic journals. I have overlaid onto these my reflective practice as a leader and as a leadership development consultant. I have explored what it is that leaders do to create sustainable superior performance - which doesn't burn people out. My findings are not a formula for successful leadership as that would be simplistic. Instead they propose conditions for human growth in the workplace which, when persisted with, are more likely to produce sustainable high performance returns.

They are conditions which are in sympathy with human nature – in the same way that organic farmers work with physical nature. They understand how to identify natural cycles, use natural materials and have patience to allow things to develop at their own speed. An organic approach to leadership is similar and demands commitment and understanding from its practitioners. It is a values-based leadership approach which wants a tangible return on investment but rejects intensive practices which overwork the resources or use unnatural accelerators. It is sustainable because it distributes leadership throughout the organisation appropriate to the task in hand. Leaders spread 'seeds' wherever they go. These can be seeds of new thoughts about change or possible futures; seeds about high performance working; seeds about teamwork or leadership growth; seeds about personal development. Leaders who follow an organic approach to leadership understand that seeds take time to grow and they know that not all seeds will take root.

In the Bible the prophet Jesus (pbuh) told a story about a man who sowed seeds.

'Then he told them many things in parables, saying: "A farmer went out to sow his seed. As he was scattering the seed, some fell along the path, and the birds came and ate it up. Some fell on rocky places, where it did not have much soil. It sprang up quickly, because the soil was shallow. But when the sun came

up, the plants were scorched, and they withered because they had no root. Other seed fell among thorns, which grew up and choked the plants. Still other seed fell on good soil, where it produced a crop - a hundred, sixty or thirty times what was sown. Whoever has ears, let them hear.'

(Matthew 13:3-9, NIV)

The high performance leader is planting seeds which will produce a bountiful crop. Not everyone they lead will hear the high performance message or want to co-operate. That is their choice. But in those that choose this different way to work there will be an outstanding crop of results. More than you can imagine. I can be sure of this not just because I have studied it but also because I have seen it emerge time and again in teams I led.

Francis Bacon wrote 'God Almighty first planted a garden'. In our work as leaders we can use the metaphor of gardening to help us understand the processes involved in developing and growing people. Psychologist Carl Rogers (1959) believed that humans have a basic motive to self-actualize - which is to fulfill one's potential and achieve the highest level of 'human-beingness'. His concept was that, just as a flower will grow to its full potential if the conditions are right, so people will flourish and reach their full potential if their environment is good enough. Flowers (and people) can be constrained by their environment. It is the job of the leader to pay attention to the environment of the workplace to make sure that the conditions are optimised for growth. Then they can stand back and watch amazing growth happen.

'The task of leadership is not to put greatness into humanity, but to elicit it, for the greatness is already there'

(John Buchan cited in Adair, 2018)

Leaders who follow such an organic approach to high performance leadership value their people. They are leaders who are authentic in their practice. They are people who believe in developing leadership capacity at every level of their organisation whether that is commercial, not for profit, faith-based, voluntary sector, large or small, private or public.

Organic leaders change things. For good.

❧ Creating The Conditions For Growth

I have talked to hundreds of business leaders during the last few years, firstly as Director of Skills & Workforce Development for the Learning & Skills Council in central London and subsequently as an independent consultant. In the corporate world I heard a common complaint that there is no longer a psychological contract between employer and employee, which makes it hard to recruit and retain talented workers. Their response is to put in place talent management strategies to encourage longer term commitment from senior employees. However this ignores the reality that in job interviews it is often *employers* who are being interviewed and chosen by talented employees in many knowledge-based, service economies. And if organisational values conflict with their personal values then people move on. Futurists now predict up to 13 career changes for an individual entering today's labour market. These are career shifts not just job moves. Our children will be doing jobs which haven't yet been invented, using technology which doesn't exist today, to solve as yet unknown problems.

Yet we persist in using recruitment techniques based on the notion that power lies with the organisation. Huge effort is made in assessment centres and behavioural interviews to discover the 'right' candidate who can then be inducted and 'on-boarded' into the organisation. Resources are expended grooming these talented individuals for top jobs based in part on their ability to fit in to the dominant culture. We have created a generation of politically astute leaders who are highly skilled in surviving the next reorganisation, downsizing or transformational programme. These leaders more often hit their targets but miss the point.

'It doesn't make sense to hire smart people and then tell them what to do. We hire smart people so they can tell us what to do.'

(Steve Jobs, 2011)

Some Corporations are particularly skilled in getting rid of the very people who can make the transformations desperately needed in their workplace. These are the leaders who can re-establish the psychological contract which has been damaged through badly managed redundancies, broken promises or a headlong rush for next quarter's profits. They are the leaders who are trustworthy. They are often the organic leaders. But the trouble is they just don't 'fit in' to the dominant culture. These organic leaders cannot help themselves wanting to change things for the better and as they do this the parent organisation senses an invasion of outside organisms and works to expel the unwelcome presence. Organic leaders create islands of excellence in their teams and departments but without more senior sponsors the prevailing culture will eventually win over and 'normal' performance resumes when the high performance, organic leader moves on.

This pattern of dysfunctional organisational behaviour should keep Chief Executives awake at night. Defending the status quo is the last thing CEO's would claim they do but in their promotion of 'best fit' candidates they often contradict themselves. Creating compatible senior teams who understand 'the way we do things around here' is a disastrous option. It dilutes leadership and builds 'good enough' cultures which can become toxic to high performance. These organisational cultures 'satisfice' at the price of organisational excellence.

The truth is we live in an uncertain world. Oil prices are volatile. The global economy has competitors like China, India and Brazil challenging established players and consuming energy which the West foolishly thought was 'ours'. Global warming is changing the climate we live in. The collapse of communism in the Soviet Union and the enlargement of the EU have altered trading relationships across Europe. Brexit will disrupt things even more. A traveller on the London tube can hear any of 200 languages spoken. Liberalised markets, deregulated industries, free flowing capital and labour are all causing change. New conflicts arise across the globe. We are experiencing huge movements of people – displaced through conflict, economic crisis, hunger, climate change or simply seeking to better their lives.

It is a confusing and unstable world. Organisations can also be confusing and unstable places to work. Organisational leaders can feel personally confused and challenged.

The skills that got you the job are not the skills you need to succeed in the job…… and that's scary.

In my conversations with leaders of small and medium sized organisations (SMEs), I hear concerns that if they train their people they will leave. Some said that communication in their business used to be good until the company expanded to 30 people and now it is too big a group for them to know everything that is going on. The very passion which created the enterprise has become the inhibitor of growth – the founder's drive to grow has transformed into excessive control which is strangling the talents of the employees. So those employees either adjust their expectations or leave, reinforcing the owner's belief that training them was indeed a bad idea. What is needed is a mirror to be held up to the owner so they see what it is like to work for them.

The skills that helped you create the business are not the skills you need to succeed in the business….. and that's scary.

Some SME leaders see and understand this point of transition and sell their business. They know they don't want to make the personal change from creative entrepreneur to a wider leadership role so they simply sell their business, move on and repeat their proven business start-up process. That is sufficient reward for them. Others see what is needed but refuse to sell or change. Their business goes into steady state but never gets beyond 25-30 people because that is the maximum span of control which can be exercised by one powerful owner. Still others get through this first control barrier but hit another one at about 250-300 people. Loss of role identity and the fear of becoming 'a Corporate' are limiting forces. Fundamentally, these are issues of leadership. How can you create the buzz of being in a small business when you are part of something much larger? It is possible.

Some uncertainties are common to both the corporate world and SMEs. Cash flow is the lifeblood of any private enterprise, client satisfaction a mantra. Selling takes place for today, tomorrow and next year as does creating profitable contracts and ceaselessly networking. But as they grow, organisations inject themselves with new uncertainties – called *people*. And the more talented the people, the greater the uncertainty!

- Entrepreneurs work best with talent that is their own.
- High performance leaders work best with talent which is *not* their own.

❧ Show me (a case study on high performance)

By Tony Nelson

This is the story of how a central London public service department was changed into a high performance team, raising the number of training interventions in London's businesses by 621% and reducing unit costs of delivery by 79%. Leaders were trained, empowered, their people equipped and we then 'got out of their way' (Nelson & Peel, 2005).

The Learning & Skills Council (LSC) was part of a £9bn national government organisation responsible for planning and funding vocational training for adults and young people in England. Central London LSC was one of 47 areas focussed on meeting the skills needs of the local economy, investing over £320m of public money annually through training providers and Colleges. The central London economy is the most complex in Europe with at that time 130,000 employers and 1.5m employees. It is the location of choice for many International and UK headquarters, central Government and a multiplicity of small and medium sized businesses. I realised that if we got the skills investment right we would see an economic impact well beyond the geographical boundaries we served. That challenge could only be met by creating a LSC Skills and Workforce Development team which was as dynamic as its customer base.

I joined central London LSC in late 2003 as Skills & Workforce Development Director. I had been brought in by Executive Director Jacqui Henderson to focus on improving work with employers. I quickly realised that the Skills Directorate was a reactive body, with a 'cheque-book' approach to investing public funds. As my Directorate members were approached by innovative private training providers they would earmark funds for small-scale interventions – up to 100 schemes were underway at any one time. Faced with a wad of papers to approve a scheme for just £300 I said we had to stop. What was required was a strategic approach to skills investment which would make a sustainable difference to workplaces across central London. This needed two things - a strategy and then a team equipped to deliver that strategy. The Directorate was dysfunctional and demoralised and was not working as a team. They would require high order influencing skills to operate collaboratively across complex partnerships and networks.

Creating the strategy was the relatively easy piece of work through 2004/5 and this was achieved through the use of open space groups using consultation with external stakeholders and internal focus groups. The truly innovative parallel piece of work was creating the conditions in which Directorate members could quickly become a team and then allow high performance to emerge and flourish. This meant working on open communication, trust, and team dynamics. Next followed equipping team members with advanced personal influencing skills to support strategic networking, partnership working and relationship building with stakeholders. I commissioned training consultant Dave Peel to design and co-deliver with me a high performance programme, to give my people a shared set of models and language for understanding the changes they were experiencing. We had worked together on a similar programme in another organisation so we both believed this would work again, albeit in a different culture.

As the high performance culture change programme continued team members found they had more choices available to them when selecting appropriate behaviours in their new roles. Managers were trained in coaching skills to support the multiple transitions involved. I needed to raise the gaze of my people - to focus them on *why* we were investing millions of pounds of public money. This purchasing power had to be used to re-shape the publicly funded vocational training market. This market was not delivering what employers said they needed in their workforces. The transformation of the Directorate into a powerful, strategic investor had to first happen *in the minds* of my thirty staff.

In parallel to this change of thinking ran the requirement to re-engineer our routes to market. We could create the capacity for working at a higher level if we contracted out hands-on activities, which included workforce development advice to employers, support for achieving Investors in People status and 'brokering' training solutions between time-starved employers and suitable training providers. As well as delivering all this change, I was tasked with making staffing reductions of 20%. So the challenges were: change the Directorate's purpose; raise aspirations and expectations; improve the distribution channels; increase the quality and reach of the service; equip the staff for high performance; and make significant cost reductions - all at the same time! This was achieved through building a clear strategic intent, making that understandable, building high performance capability in depth and then getting out of the way of the high performance team.

The programme involved six intensive workshops over an 18 month period between 2004 and 2005. Managers, and subsequently many team members, were trained in coaching skills. 88% of team members and 100% of managers in evaluation reported increased effectiveness, with triangulated favourable comments from external stakeholders. This was despite the challenge of new people joining the team whilst the programme was running. Communication within the team showed a marked shift from the benchmarked scores with a 300% improvement. Trust levels went from 23% low/77% medium to an astonishing 71% medium/29% high. In the training 78% of delegates thought their personal understanding of change had developed. Motivation levels increased by 54% and 71% of people reported an improvement in their influencing skills. In an independent LSC Employee Opinion Survey in 2005 the Directorate scored significantly higher than the average of the other central London departments - trust was +6% above average, with focus on learning +19%, and communication +9%.

By putting into practice the skills learned on the programme the Directorate was able to support an additional 81 employers to achieve coveted Investors in People status. They also raised the total number of 'other employers assisted with training' from 227 to 1312. External stakeholders showered praise. The London Development Agency said 'A lot more focused... a much more pro-active partner'; a training provider observed 'The relationship has strengthened'; a FE College said we were 'more open and transparent'; a stakeholder reported we now 'resolve issues...and are more focussed'; and two training providers said 'there has been a change of attitude' and they 'actively listened to us'.

Lessons learned
- It is essential that the most senior manager personally role models the changes required, so that theory becomes practice quickly
- It takes courage and resilience to continue once the organisational cynics get warmed up - but we saw even the cynics converted and become enthusiastic champions in time. Don't give up. Be patient.
- Maintain the momentum - interrupting the training will cause a loss of traction. The first 18 months is vital.
- Build team capacity to take ownership of its own development - integrating coaching skills is essential for this. It also maximises value for money and return on investment.

In 2005 the high performance programme won a prestigious National Training Award which served to re-energise the team due to wider external recognition gained.

➤ High Performance Literature Review
Our minds thrive on making connections in order to make patterns out of our experiences but John Paul Getty is reported to have said 'in times of rapid change, experience could be your worst enemy'. Getty realised that our search for making patterns can become a weakness in times of accelerated change and instability. Lucas (2010) wrote that we may need to *unlearn* things and get better at developing more rewarding and shorter-term relationships. He felt it was necessary to imagine the future and reframe situations, developing our 'adaptive intelligence'. The pursuit of high performance calls for a re-wiring of our brains to see learning and unlearning as a continuous, reflexive process.

*'The illiterate of the 21st century will not be those who can-
not read and write, but those who cannot learn, unlearn
and relearn'*

(Toffler, 1984)

High performance teams need social glue. Mark De Rond
(2009) is a Professor of Organizational Ethnography at Cambridge
University who lived with a team from Cambridge University as
they prepared for the Oxford- Cambridge boat race in 2007. He
studied first-hand what it was like to be part of this high performance environment. One of his findings concerned the social glue
needed to make such a team effective. In this team a man called
Dan 'was the one who seems to supply that key ingredient that ce-
ments them into a crew as opposed to a band of eight outrageous-
ly talented but dysfunctional individuals'. As the race approached
the coaches had to choose from a bigger squad the final eight who
would row the race on the river Thames. Dan was not in that eight.
However, the rowers who had been selected realised that they could
not win the race without him. They believed that excluding Dan
was a mistake so great they were willing to risk any consequence
of challenging the coaches' final decision. On the metrics Dan was
not the strongest rower and the coaches had selected a team of
eight who were the fittest and strongest. It was the rowers themselves, and not the coaches, who knew the true value of Dan lay not
in his rowing but in his social contribution to the team. De Rond
wrote 'by helping the crew to lighten up and bond, to be able to
find the silver lining around even the gloomiest cloud, Dan seemed
uniquely capable of ensuring that the crew would work effectively
as a unit'. The coaches listened to the arguments to include Dan in
the final team and wisely revisited their decision. *They were willing
to travel their unlearning curve.* They changed their decision and
included Dan in the final eight. It proved to be the right decision,
as that crew went on to win the race.

High performance needs a change of mindset. In a lecture for the LSC in December 2004 in London Mark England, Games Services Director of the British Olympic Association, described the high performance environment of the England Olympic squad as athletes 'raising the bar on their own performance'. Sir Clive Woodward coached the England rugby team to win the 2003 Rugby World Cup. He had a successful business career before taking on his coaching role and brought to the task the philosophy he had developed.

> *'Inherited thinking is a curse. So before we do anything, we have to change the way we think'*

> *(Woodward, 2004)*

Woodward developed a model to take the England Rugby team to world class performance. He centred this on getting team fundamentals in place, building superb coaching systems and creating an experience of elite working to change the mindset of his players. He realised the way to release their potential was in changing their thought patterns - raising aspiration and challenging the old ways of doing things. This was a process of setting new, demanding standards which were owned by the whole team. As he rebuilt the England rugby team he knew he needed to change the way they saw themselves and the way they viewed their team. One of his innovations was to take them to visit high performance environments so that they could 'touch the future'. He wanted them to see and feel what such high performance teams were like. They spent a few days with the Royal Marines at their training facility in south west England. It was an exhausting and demanding experience. They were put through their paces by senior non-commissioned officers (NCO's) who were responsible for training and selecting future Royal Marines. They were expert in assessing aptitude and people's lives rested on them making correct decisions. Royal Marine teams operate all over the world in high risk combat situations in which every member of the team has to be able to function reliably under intense pressure. As the rugby squad were returning by helicopter to the Marines base at the end of their immersive training, Woodward asked the NCO's who they thought should not be in the England rugby squad. This was the moment the NCO's had been waiting for and the answer surprised Woodward. The NCO's had identified an individual who they said was an emotional 'energy sapper' in the squad. Such an individual sucked the energy out of the group and in their environment would not be passed as successful as a Marine, even if all the other technical and physical performance indicators were OK. Woodward was shocked because he knew this individual was one of his best players. He reflected carefully on return to Twickenham and came to understand the wisdom of what he had been told. He dropped that individual from the England team. He realised he needed to highly value team impact and dynamics more highly.

Cultures that nurture high performance

Gratton (2007) studied what she called 'Hot Spots' in organisations around the world. Gratton wrote that these centres of intense energy make people feel 'energized and vibrantly alive. Your brain is buzzing with ideas and the people around you share your joy and excitement. The energy is palpable, bright and shining. These are times when what you and others have always known becomes clearer, when adding value becomes more possible.' She is describing high performance team culture. Hot Spots are 'an emergent phenomena that cannot be controlled or directed. Executives influence the emergence of Hot Spots by shaping context…'. The release of this latent energy is the result of a dynamic combination of four elements:

- A cooperative mindset
- Boundary spanning

- Igniting purpose
- Productive capacity

We will explore these elements of high performance culture within the high performance team model in the next chapter. Hofstede and Hofstede (2005) call patterns of thinking, feeling and acting *mental software* which is more commonly termed culture. They write 'this word (culture) has several meanings, all derived from its Latin source, which refers to the tilling of the soil'. I believe that leaders who enable high performance culture to emerge are tilling the 'soil' of the human mind.

Perhaps the biggest challenge for CEOs is to create the organisational climate in which high performance can flourish. Handy (1976) recommends 'more trust and less control, more diversity and less uniformity, more differentiation and less systemization'. A key seems to be to work within the existing culture of an organisation to promote effective teams to deliver the organisation's products or services. Interestingly, Katzenbach and Smith (1993) note that top teams are the most difficult, with 'ingrained individualism'. They say that organisations which aspire to high performance may need to look closely at top team performance - or recognise consciously that they are led by a working group rather than a team. Katzenbach and Smith (1998) write that 'real teams at the top happen naturally only when a major, unexpected event forces the issue - and only when the instincts of the senior leader permit the discipline of team performance to be applied'. Bion (1991) writes 'the group is the place where we play out our inner psychological lives – a group's decisions will reflect those psychological realities.... but for a top team, the stakes are bigger'. Johnson (1988) in a paper exploring Boards writes 'significant gaps in our understanding remains' about the contribution which boards make to organisational performance but 'the creative potential of groups is more than the sum of their parts'. Goleman et al (2003) writes 'more than anyone else, it is the team leader who has the power to establish norms' and that setting the right ground rules is 'common sense but not common practice'.

Focusing on the creation and maintenance of high performance teams (HPT) will in itself change the wider organisational culture over time. These teams need to be highly task focused with clear goals, high standards and be greatly valued by the organisation's leaders. They should be commissioned to make things better or do better things. 'Cultivating a few real teams is one of the best ways of upgrading the overall performance ethic of an organisation' (Katzenbach and Smith, 1993) who say that teams 'contribute so much to major organisational transformations' because of their 'link between performance and behaviour change'. Interestingly, Bevan et al (2005) found that 'the exact (organisational) structure and shape deployed seems to make little difference to high performing organisations'. They go on to say that bureaucracies obsess over structure but in high performing organisations 'no single organisational design seemed to emerge'.

Handy (1976) states organisations share one of four dominant cultures in organisations – power, role, task or person based – with the task culture described as a 'team culture'. He implies the task (team) culture is closest to a high performance culture and sees it as extremely flexible - 'you will find the task (team) culture where the market is competitive, where the product life is short, where speed of reaction is important'. Katzenbach and Smith (1993) suggest that successful organisations are moving towards organisational designs that are 'simpler and more flexible' than command and control; 'organize around processes instead of functions'; and 'emphasise teams as the key performance unit'. Significantly they 'think it is fair to say that teams are a microcosm of the high performance organisation itself'. In a sense they are describing a team culture as the one most likely to foster high performance working – this expresses an idea of high performance coming not from rigid structure but from looser, group working. The high performance literature points to a strong correlation between organisational high performance and the use of effective teams as a mutually reinforcing model of excellence.

Rajan (1996) identifies four types of business culture in the organisations he studied: Caring (relationship driven), Formal (rules driven), Progressive (excellence driven) and Entrepreneurial (performance driven). The latter two were more likely in his view to promote teamwork. These relate well to Handy's Task and Power cultures. Rajan (2004a) says that in the private sector 'the overwhelming emphasis has been to change the employee mindset from a loyal servant to a committed worker' to create a high performance environment whereas in the public sector the emphasis has been to take service development 'from rigidity to flexibility'. The 'mindset shift' associated with high performance according to Rajan is:

Paternalism	TO	Performance
Entitlement	TO	Self-employment
Rigidity	TO	Agility
Blame culture	TO	Personal accountability
Weak Management	TO	Strong Leadership

Rajan (2004b) uses the metaphor of jazz to describe leadership in a high performance organisation: jazz band leaders bring together a talented group of musicians but 'the music comes from something we cannot direct, from a unified whole created among the players'. In a study of 850 UK companies who had all been recognised by the Design Council as innovative in the previous five years, several factors for success were found in the top performers (The Talent Foundation, 2001). The leadership style in these top performing organisations showed that leaders create the climate for 'staff to reach the best answer themselves' and displayed high levels of trust. They were 'clear about where they want their organisation to go - and good at inspiring their people to reach it.' The study found 'people who work for top performers know that their managers and team leaders take an interest in them as individuals'. Bolman and Deal (1997) write 'many highly successful organisations (are) investing in people on the premise that a highly motivated and skilled workforce is a powerful competitive advantage'.

Pfeffer (1998) writes 'I have observed three basic principles that leaders use to transform their organisations to a high commitment model of management: build trust, encourage change and use appropriate measures of performance'. Heskett and Schlesinger (in Hesselbein et al, 1996) studied high performance organisations in the U.S.A. and observed that these leaders used inspirational language, listened a lot, articulated clear core values, lived the values they espoused, developed employee's capability and treated people with dignity. They believe that culture, leadership and high performance are inextricably intertwined. Bevan et al (2005) in a study of high performing firms found some 'clear cultural norms'. These included a 'distrust of the status quo, valuing quality over quantity, external and internal focus and a sense of pride'. Critically important was 'allowing workers as much control as possible over when, where and how the job is done'. The organisations studied had 'equal measures of task and people orientation'. Goleman et al (2003) write that a leader's words are contagious, so leaders need to develop their emotional intelligence (EI), writing that 'emotional leadership is the spark that ignites a company's performance' and 'high levels of EI in a leader are associated with climates where high performance is more likely'. Conversely they state 'low levels of EI in a leader are associated with toxic climates (fear, anxiety)'. Goleman et al describe the emotionally intelligent leader as one who can monitor his moods (self-awareness); change them for the better (self- management); understand their impact (empathy); and act in ways that boost other's moods (relationship management).

There is no organisational culture which is the best fit for high performance in every situation. What does seem to be vitally important, however, in creating high performance in organisations is teamwork – the culture needs to be one in which teams can flourish with high levels of trust and an embracing of change through flexible patterns of work, thinking and expressions.

How high performing teams occur

Katzenbach and Smith (2004) observe 'the critical role for senior managers. .. is to worry about company performance and the kinds of teams that can deliver it'. They argue that a team has a 'unique potential to deliver results' and leaders should 'foster the basic discipline of teams'. It is in doing so that 'top management creates the kind of environment that enables team, as well as individual and organisational, performance'. Katzenbach and Smith advise ' the wisest leaders will do whatever it takes, from providing recognition or additional challenges to just getting out of the way, to keep these valuable teams – and all they represent and influence – alive'.

All teams need to go through a building process. Tuckman and Jensen (1977) argue that teams go through five stages of forming, storming, norming, performing and adjourning. A group has to go through these stages consecutively but may stick at any stage if members are unwilling to develop. Beech et al (2001) writes 'Tuckman's work is most effective when groups reach stage three of development. At this point, the members have experienced stages one and two and are in a receptive mode to take on board the implications of stage four'. However Beech points out that not all groups reach this stage. For those that do 'there is unity: group identity is complete, group morale is high, and group loyalty is intense'. Handy (1976) writes 'when the task is very important, when the individuals are highly committed to the group, or when individual and group objectives are identical then these stages may become almost perfunctory'. This appears to be describing the rapid formation of a high performance team.

The Leadership Trust condensed Tuckman's model into four stages – Form, Storm, Reform, Perform – 'we prefer to use the word reform as opposed to norm as it better describes the challenge of re-grouping that leaders are ultimately responsible for overseeing' writes Edwards et al (2002). The goal of high performance is what a leader needs to have in mind when leading a team's development and growth – a journey of excellent results, first class relationships and open communication. Katzenbach and Smith (1993) write that high performing teams emerge and are rare because of the intense commitment needed amongst members of such teams.

Leadership styles to encourage high performance
It might be expected that some leadership styles are more likely than others to produce a high performance culture. Effective leadership of teams is essential to setting the scene for high performance (Katzenbach and Smith, 2004) because teams are 'essential to organisational effectiveness'.

The scientific Taylorist approach to management stifled creativity but maximised productivity, in an overemphasis on 'Task' using Adair's terminology. In today's knowledge-based, service economy the conditions for creating and sustaining high performance must address the needs of team members who are well-educated. Their needs are high order: 'talented, productive people are being thwarted ...by gaps in emotional intelligence – in themselves, (and) their bosses' (Cooper and Sawaf, 1997). Huxham and Beech (2003) describe high performance workplaces deriving decisions 'throughout the hierarchy' i.e. an *involved* workforce. High performance leaders address the emotional climate of their team. Lawlor (2004) writes about leadership in high performance organisations and the importance of creating a 'leadership brand' to provide consistency of leadership approach across the organisation, 'It should not involve what is often called situational leadership…employees do not want to be uncertain about how they will be treated'. Sharman (1997) observes 'a new type of team is emerging that is more fluid and flexible than in the past… and it is the task of the leader to ensure that the output of the group is more than the sum of its parts. This means…real, effective, proactive teamwork, which enables every member of the team to contribute to their full potential'.

Handy (1976) suggests that 'a powerful leader has a positive effect on the morale of the work group. People like working under a respected chief.' Handy suggests that high producing groups are associated with leaders being able to influence upwards. This points to high performance teams having tasks perceived as important and a leader perceived as powerful by both the team and outside it. Horne and Stedman Jones (2001) stress the importance of a leader inspiring their team and that 'successful leaders are those who learn to share (challenges) by empowering and trusting their teams'. Adair (2003b) writes 'a leader is a dealer in hope'. Jurgen Klopp has created a highly successful Premier League football team at Liverpool. He was interviewed about his approach to leadership and said this:

'We have enough confidence and that's very important for a leader. If I would expect from myself that I know everything and I'm the best in everything, I couldn't have confidence. But I don't expect that. I know I'm good in a couple of things, really good in a few things, and that's enough. My confidence is big enough that I can really let people grow next to me, it's no problem. I need experts around me. It's really very important that you are empathetic, that you try to understand the people around you, and that you give real support to the people around you. Then everybody can act.

That's what leadership is: have strong people around you with a better knowledge in different departments than your-

*self, don't act like you know everything, be ready to admit, 'I
have no clue in the moment, give me a couple of minutes and
then I will have a clue probably.'*

(Klopp in Shaw, 2019)

Jones et al (1996) drawing from Burns (1978) suggest a transformational leadership style is more likely to develop the characteristics of high performance in organisations and teams: 'It works
to help all parties achieve greater motivation, satisfaction and a
greater sense of achievement. It requires trust, concern and facili-
tation rather than direct control. The skills required are concerned
with establishing a long term vision, empowering people to control
themselves, coaching and developing others and challenging the
culture to change', (Jones et al 1996). Jones contrasts this with transactional leadership which 'depends on hierarchy and the ability to
work through the mode of exchange. It requires leadership skills...
to obtain results, to control through structures and processes, to
solve problems, to plan and organize, and work within the structures and boundaries of the organisation'. Gill (2001) writes 'transformational leaders dramatically change people's expectations
about themselves. And they achieve much greater motivation and
performance in their subordinates or followers than laissez-faire
and transactional leaders do'. Gill goes on 'research at the Leadership Trust suggests that transactional leaders are primarily directive...while the more effective transformational leaders use the
directive, consultative, participative and delegative styles' which
is a more holistic approach. However Gill warns 'current thinking
about transformational leadership needs to be expanded .... (as
it is) weak on the formulation of vision and strategy'. He explains
'effective leaders communicate a rational, appealing vision of the
future and show the way through strategies' as 'without strategies,
vision is a dream'. Gill adds 'leaders who create a leadership brand
in their organisations through vision, strategy, shared values, em-

powerment and inspiration will transform the expectations and achievements of their people'. Al-Azami (2019), drawing on the work of Banna, writes that leaders should apply the Islamic principle of *tayyib* (best practice standards) to their situations rather than the bare minimum standards of *halal*. In other words leaders should seek excellence in themselves and those they lead and that this approach is an outworking of their belief system.

The Groupthink dilemma

High performance teams will display a high degree of social cohesion and group loyalty. This can place the team in a dilemma which Janis (1982a) describes as 'groupthink'. He defines this as 'a deterioration of mental efficiency, reality testing, and moral judgement that results from in-group pressures'. Beekun and Badawi (2009) say that in groupthink:

> *'The process of shura (consultation) may be distorted. If the leader surrounds himself by unquestioning members, the outcome of the consultative process will be limited to validating his decisions. The drive for consensus and simultaneous suppression of dissent is known as groupthink'.*

Garvin and Roberto (2001) describe the importance of 'advocacy versus enquiry' in action, citing the Bay of Pigs disaster contrasted with the later Cuban Missile Crisis. President Kennedy is shown to have adopted some of these Groupthink prevention techniques to promote effective team work in the Cuban crisis avoiding the earlier procedural weaknesses evident in the Bay of Pigs incident. Handy (1976) quotes Janis summarising these changes by Kennedy as introducing 'a more diffuse group, more outside ideas, more testing of alternatives and more sensitivity to conflicting data'. President Kennedy and his brother Robert built a high performance team on the group dynamics lessons they had experientially learned during the Bay of Pigs disaster.

A cohesive group can overestimate its power or mortality, display closed-mindedness and pressurise members towards conformity. Groupthink occurs when the team leader focuses primarily on the quality of relationships and not also on the quality of decisions. This leads to consensus decisions. These groups ensure feedback is always comfortable. High Performance teams can help avoid groupthink by deliberately promoting challenge within the group in order to test and develop better thinking. The more socially cohesive a group is the greater the danger of groupthink as the pressure becomes intense to conform to group norms and ideas. Groupthink culture is an intellectually toxic environment and is the antithesis of high performance culture. Handy (1976) writes that just being out of alignment with a group places a member under intense pressure to conform. He continues, there is evidence that 'heterogeneous groups tend to exhibit more conflict, but most studies do show them to be more productive than the homogeneous groups'. However as tasks become more complex the issue of compatibility becomes more important so Handy's implication is that HPTs need to be trained to avoid groupthink. Janis (1982a) wrote that if relationships rule, challenge is banished in a group. Work then becomes a cosy club. This is a dangerous place which promotes 'a mode of thinking that people engage in when they are deeply involved in a cohesive group, when the members' strivings for unanimity override their motivation to realistically appraise alternative courses of action'.

Measurement in high performance organisations

Pfeffer (1998) writes of how traditional financial reporting systems go into great detail about 'what *has* happened' but the need is for systems to measure the drivers of success. Pfeffer says 'it is the job of management to lead a process in which key success factors are understood, measurements for them developed, and then attention focused on those measures'. This is so that 'their measurement systems contribute rather than cause problems'. Many high performance, world class, organisations use a Balanced Scorecard approach as proposed by Kaplan and Norton (1992) to manage their results holistically across a basket of a few key measures. Organisations using a Balanced Scorecard recognise that unintended consequences happen in complex systems. They manage like a 'plate spinner' paying attention to those plates which matter. It takes time for a high performance organisation to develop the right measures to use on its scorecard but this 'should not be cut short, as it develops alignment and a common understanding of the strategy' (Jones et al 1996).

The obsession in some organisations to pursue dozens of targets produces results in one area which are then offset by unintended consequences elsewhere. In the UK's National Health Service, for example, Health Ministers have reduced problems to measurement by a single target but 'in order for decomposition to work as a problem solving strategy, the problem world must not be tightly interconnected' (March, 1994). This could be why the NHS is not a high performing organisation. Fuller et al (2003) write that the imposition of central targets on NHS Trusts can divert senior managers away from their more important task of promoting high performance through informal team learning. Katzenbach and Smith (1993) set out three dimensions for a 'balanced performance ethic satisfying shareholders, customers and employees'. Work done by Collins and Porras (1994) underlines the importance of organisations developing holistic measures of success. 'A stunning outcome from Collins and Porras's research is that companies that emphasise values beyond the bottom line were more profitable in the long run than companies who stated their goals in purely financial terms' (Bolman and Deal, 1997).

Harding et al (2003) developed a High Performance Index from a study of over 1000 high performing UK companies and defined five strategic factors which, when effectively developed and managed, are strongly associated with superior performance. These were Customers and markets; Shareholders and governance; Stakeholders; HR practices and Creativity and Innovation Management. 'High performing companies do not perform in just one of these areas – they must perform in all of them'. They do not take a narrow view of performance. In a follow up study (Bevan et al, 2005), the Work Foundation used the index above and measured performance in 3000 firms over a year. The research showed that 'the top third of firms out-perform the bottom two-thirds by £1600 per worker per annum' using index criteria. The study showed high performance work practices 'had more impact when implemented in bundles rather than in isolation' and that higher performing firms adopted a pragmatic 'contingency' approach to the combination of business goals and the practices they chose to achieve them. In the low performing organisations in this study leadership discussion 'focused more on what the numbers say rather than how top managers behave and interact with others'.

Bringing culture and leadership together

High Performance culture seems to be a product of actions taken by leaders to promote effective team work, using a few key performance indicators which are carefully chosen. Such a culture is more likely to occur in an organisation with a sharp focus on performance, which is flexible, open to change, and uses project working. High performance organisations are future focused, have clear direction and employees feel valued. Trust is high in these organisations.

A key building block of high performance is the team. In high performance environments they are no bigger than about 25 people, have clear common purpose and goals, strong task focus and performance measures they have developed themselves. It is not the team which is their focus but the tasks and team standards – they carry no 'passengers'. Their leaders use metaphor and give meaning. Leadership is shared around team members and the formal leader manages superbly the boundary between the team and the wider organisation. These leaders use their personal power rather than positional authority. They understand and address the emotional issues which drive and sustain high performance. The needs of stakeholders, customers and team members are met.

High performance teams feel different to normal teams – key words are urgency, action, feedback, commitment, trust, challenge, emotion, conflict, communication and coaching. High performance teams have important tasks and powerful leaders but the leader builds capability rather than dependence. High performance teams learn from themselves, from others, from their environment and from their results. Membership of a high performance team is an almost spiritual experience with intense loyalty, focus and emotion. These teams occur when leaders give them space and team members step up to the opportunity. They push through barriers and guard against groupthink.

There are many definitions of high performance but one I especially like is

A high performance team is *'one that outperforms all other like teams, and outperforms expectations given its composition'*

(Katzenbach & Smith, 1993)

Reflecting on High Performance
Take a few minutes to think about the following questions and write down your answers drawing on your experiences and insights.
- What does 'high performance' mean for you?
- Have you experienced it?
- What did it feel like?

Now imagine for a moment that high performance working is in place right across your team at work. What would you be noticing? What would others be noticing?

❧ **The key leadership wisdom from reviewing the journey toward high performance is:**

- Catching people 'doing things right' is more powerful than catching them doing things wrong
- A leader can create the conditions in which high performance can naturally emerge
- These conditions are defined by a set of leadership actions which together create a facilitating culture
- My award-winning high performance model has been used successfully in the UK and Iraq, with teams large and small, public and private sector, across organisational boundaries and national cultures
- High performance is an organic principle
- High performance occurs as individual people and teams 'self-actualise' (achieve their full potential)
- High performance leaders work best with talent that is not their own
- High performance is caught not taught – the top leader has to role model the behaviours to their team
- High performance takes courage and resilience to lead
- Building team capacity through coaching is essential for the team to own its development
- High performance is a mindset shift and almost a spiritual experience

CHAPTER 8

Leadership wisdom to create high performance

❧ PART TWO: **The high performance model**
I created this high performance model from the answers I discovered to my Big Question: what is it that leaders do to create and sustain high performance? The five compelling themes that leaders of high performance pay attention to are Adaptability, Leadership, Focus, Openness and Reputation.

High Performance Team model (Nelson, 2010 adapted)

~❧ FOCUS

A high performing team has a sharp focus.

Clear and urgent team purpose with high energy and passion

A high performing team knows why it exists – it has a clear reason for being. It is not there by accident. If a visitor were to ask people across the team about that purpose they would receive consistent answers. There is high energy and tangible passion (a 'buzz') to its work which people can feel. The leader of a high performance team pays attention to the energy levels of team members.

Structure is used to team advantage

The evidence points to a maximum HPT size of no more than about 25 members - ideally below 15 (Katzenbach and Smith, 2004). Once a team becomes too large it naturally starts to break down into sub teams (Handy, 1976). This reflects the need for people to be in groups in which they feel psychologically and emotionally safe and are able to get to know the other team members. It is not possible to do that in a very large group. The team leader ensures that the team's organisational structure is not getting in the way of high performance working.

In a study of a high performing US Army Special Forces team, researchers identified the reason for its success as 'its ability to reconfigure depending on the situation. Planning for missions, the group functioned democratically (but) executing the plan was another story. The group's structure changed from a loose creative confederation to a well-defined tightly controlled chain of command,' (Bolman & Deal, 1997). This team was able to adapt its form and ways of working to the phases of the task it faced. The learning is that high performance teams must adapt to circumstances so that structure doesn't get in the way but instead is used to the team's advantage. Bolman & Deal write it is challenging to find the right structure.

In the British Special Air Service a similar, informal style of leadership also prevails:

'The SAS has a different culture, attitude and modus operandi, based on informal relationships that allow people to communicate much more openly, honestly and directly with one another. In short, their hierarchy of command is much more horizontal.'

(Gilbert-Smith, 2003)

Team develops own measures of success

A high performance team is jealous of the way it measures performance. It will set demanding targets and goals for itself and these are *in addition* to all externally imposed targets. In other words they willingly go beyond the expectations of the wider organisation and stakeholders. This 'discretionary effort' is a hallmark of high performing groups. In the UK there is much debate amongst government and business about how to improve productivity levels. Whilst the solutions to this embedded national productivity challenge are complex it is becoming increasingly accepted that the role of leadership is critical in creating a culture which supports high productivity. I have no doubt that the creation of HPT's will be a key part of the turnaround needed to support the UK economy. The old models of leadership are proving obsolete and my hope is that the emerging generation of young workers will demand better of its leadership.

The leader of a HPT has high expectations of the team's behaviours and performance – they are demanding and articulate those demands clearly. The leader understands that once a HPT is working it 'acts to set and police its own standards' (Katzenbach & Smith, 1993) and that 'real teams are much more likely to flourish if leaders aim their sights on performance results that balance the needs of customers, employees and shareholders' (in other words the stakeholders). High performance teams are usually closely involved in developing their own measures and targets to meet goals and objectives. 'Team members need to be trained in goal-setting and monitoring techniques' (Jones et al, 1996). Meyer (1994) writes of the importance of measurement to gauge success and that the 'truly empowered team must play the lead role in designing its own measurement system'. Seddon (1992) adds 'the key to continuous improvement is that measurement should be used by the people that do the work'.

The leader's role in relation to the task of the team is certainly more than just the 'ability to achieve some control over one's work' (Salaman, 1995). The leader must create a clear sense of purpose around the tasks of the team. 'A team which does not have a clearly defined goal is not a team '(Jones et al, 1996). Sometimes goals are mandated to teams, sometimes they are developed from within the team, but Jones writes 'holding a shared goal does not mean that team members must be in total agreement about how to fulfil the objective'. The leader's role is to elicit the creativity of the team so that it is the team which figures out how it fulfils the objective. Bevan et al (2005) in a study of 3000 firms found that in high performance organisations leadership was 'visible and accessible' with 'high expectations from those in decision-making roles'.

The Leadership Trust defines leadership as 'using our personal power to win the hearts and minds of those around us to achieve a common purpose'. This definition can be used to support the maintenance of high performing teams given its focus on a common purpose. The concepts of personal power and winning hearts and minds resonate with the writings of Covey (1992) who observes 'you have to build the emotional bank accounts that create commerce between hearts'. Implicit in this statement is the sense of a common, emotional, purpose between leader and follower. The Leadership Trust (2003) ask in their *Pocket Book Tutor* that leadership and followership are set at the 'highest not the lowest levels'. This means that in creating high performing teams we bring together a group 'who would quickly attain the dizzy heights of co-operation and outstanding results' (Whitmore, 2002).

Clear focus on internal customers

In a HPT, colleagues are treated as 'customers' of the service being provided. For example, someone from Finance asking for information from a Marketing colleague to support budget reporting will be treated respectfully, with their expectations managed and needs for data supply met. Promises made are kept or the relationship is protected by early warning of a likely failure to meet an agreed deadline, followed by mutually agreed renegotiation. The way internal colleagues are treated by HPT's reflects the same levels of professionalism which would be afforded to an external customer. This applies to colleagues within and across the team and to all colleagues outside the high performance environment as well.

Clear focus on external customers- exceptional results

The drive in a HPT to understand, meet and exceed the expectations of external customers is very strong. The team delights in meeting or exceeding agreed outcomes for external customers. The HPT uses a sharp and clear understanding of its Focus to shape the team's thinking, practice and outcomes.

ᕽ OPENNESS

A HPT is characterised by an extraordinary level of openness across the team. Lucas (2010) wrote 'it becomes the goal of any high performing team to get smarter at sharing its thinking patterns'. Members of this type of team are transparent with each other.

Demanding behaviour standards

High performance teams develop their own culture and Hofstede and Hofstede (2005) write:

> *'Culture is the unwritten book, with rules of the social game that is passed on to newcomers by its members, nesting itself in their minds'*

Behaviour norms are high in a HPT, set initially by the leader of the team and then increasingly the team will police its own behaviour standards. The team carries no 'passengers' (i.e. people who want to be in the team but who do not want to work hard or meet the high standards expected). Team members will seek to influence a passenger but, if no improvement is seen in their effort or contribution, it will be made increasingly clear to them that they have no place in the high performance environment. Indeed, a lazy person who finds themselves in a HPT will feel very uncomfortable with the high standards and is likely to want to extricate themselves quickly. There is one exception, which is when an established HPT member falls on hard times perhaps emotionally or with ill health – they will find that the team will carry them for as long as it takes to recover. Because they are a member who has already earned their place on the team there is no question of them being seen as a passenger; they are a respected colleague in distress and will be supported accordingly.

Bolman and Deal (1997) point out that Vaill's 1982 research on high performing groups 'concluded that spirit was at the core of every group he studied'. They go on to write 'more and more teams and organisations now realise that culture, soul and spirit are the well springs of high performance'. They go further and state 'peak performance emerges as a team discovers its soul'.

High levels of trust and commitment to each other

Morris et al (1995) emphasise the importance to winning teams of 'a sense of belonging - mutual trust'. It is not necessary to like everyone on the team but, regardless of personal chemistry, members have high trust and respect for one another. HPT members are committed not just to the team purpose but to one another. In a HPT there is no gossip or back-biting because this is seen as a destructive behaviour.

'Trust and respect are the twin pillars of leadership'

(Gilbert-Smith, 2003)

High performance teams are set apart by 'the degree of commitment, particularly how deeply committed the members are to one another' (Katzenbach and Smith, 1993). This commitment, they write, is to both one another's growth and success. A high performance team is what they call a Real Team, only more so, with a 'deeper sense of purpose, more ambitious performance goals, more complete approaches, fuller mutual accountability, interchangeable as well as complementary skills'. The scarcity of such high performing teams is, in their view, because of the 'high degree of personal commitment to one another'. The culture of these teams is a focus on 'performance and team basics'. However 'no rules, best practices, or secret formulas exist that ensure high performance outcomes'. These outcomes can be made more likely by leaders but are not guaranteed.

Beech and Crane (1999) argue that it is the 'climate of satisfaction' that is important in a high performance team, rather than more task related factors. They identified three key factors for making the transition from teamwork to high performance teams: 'transparency (the team is involved in how they are measured); checkability (the team can demonstrate achievement against realistic quantitative and qualitative measures); and the social climate of community (it is a learning culture, not a blame culture, with shared values and where conflicts are resolved effectively)'. Leadership, argue Beech and Crane comes from *within* a high performance team.

Katzenbach and Smith (2004) identified that teams want accountability translated into clear goals. And a very important part of the 'emotional logic that drives team performance' is that all team members perform equal amounts of work. The very experience of being part of an effective team was, for team members, a source of energy and motivation unlike their normal work. High performing teams become self-sufficient in their view.

The ability to build trust is key to high performance – within the team first and then outside it. The 'trust building loop' illustrates this (Huxham and Vangen, 2004). Research by the UK's Institute of Leadership and Management (2014) calculated a trust score for organisations in the U.K. It makes for sobering reading. They asked over 1600 managers from a variety of settings to score trust levels in their organisations. By adding together the positive values and subtracting the negative values it allowed them to calculate 'high net trust'. The all-industry average high net trust score was 40%. But in Financial services it was only 34%, Education 32% and in central & Local Government (including Police) a tiny 10%. Management guru Stephen Covey (2008) believes that where trust is low, change can only happen at low speed and high cost. That low trust acts like a hidden tax on an economy. In other words, leaders need to engage their workforce and generate high levels of trust in their integrity, communication and competence. Otherwise the impact of their leadership is going to drain away. Interestingly, the research found that managers have high trust towards their direct reports but lower trust of their peers or boss. And first line managers are the least trusting and trusted. All these figures get worse the larger the organisation. So what are the top five drivers of being trusted?

- Openness
- Effective communication
- Ability to make decisions
- Integrity
- Competence in their role

Leaders who are concerned about the trust deficit should seek feedback on how they are doing on these five criteria and then act on it.

Adair (2018) reflects on the vital importance of integrity in leadership:

' *The prophet Muhammad and the first four caliphs of Islam, for example, led simple lives and were scrupulous in all financial matters, and corruption was unknown in the Muslim states of their day. The first president of Botswana and his three successors set their faces against corruption, and as a result Botswana became the least corrupt nation in Africa'.*

There is open communication in the team

Dialogue within the HPT is characterised by honest communication which might be described as reality combined with dignity. Conversations are honest and frank. Team members are able to talk openly about their opinions and feelings on work, goals, concerns or team behaviour. Edwards et al (2002) describe the Leadership Trust's model of a high performing team climbing a communications pyramid with members taking increasing risks with self- disclosure: 'willingness, or otherwise, to travel up the pyramid will, to a large extent, depend on the levels of trust, honesty and openness within the team'. Lencioni (2005) says that effective teams have to engage in two types of communication but only one of these is practical in a large group:

'According to Harvard's Chris Argyris, those two types of communication are advocacy and inquiry. Basically, advocacy is the statement of ideas and opinions; inquiry is the asking of questions for clarity and understanding. When a group gets too large, people realize they are not going to get the floor back any time soon, so they resort almost exclusively to advocacy. It becomes like Congress (which is not designed to be a team) or the United Nations'.

So, to promote the most effective openness and communication it is vital to keep the team at a size which ensures that *inquiry* can be effective.

Emotional intelligence is high within the team

Goleman (2002b) develops the argument that 'the leader's fundamental task is an emotional one'. Many leaders are unaware of the emotional wake they leave behind them but leaders of HPT's are acutely aware of their emotional impact on the team. They also notice the emotional impact of others. Goleman writes 'research clearly shows that when people are angry, anxious, alienated or depressed their work suffers .... upsetting emotions are meant to be signals to pay attention to what's distressing and to do something about that'. The leader's job is to make it safe to discuss the emotional reality. Nelson Mandela said 'Don't address their brains. Address their hearts' (Carlin, 2008) when explaining how he would approach the leadership of change at a critical time in South Africa's transition from white minority rule towards his vision of a 'rainbow nation'. Mandela paid close attention to the emotional needs of those he sought to lead, including the skilled use of symbols such as the Springbok rugby team which Mandela turned into 'the embodiment not of hate and fear, but generosity and love'. Mandela had high emotional intelligence.

All HPT members use emotional intelligence to achieve the team's purpose through effective relationships. Such teams demonstrate extraordinary awareness of the emotional health both of the team overall and of individual team members. This characteristic complements the team's wider openness and commitment to excellent communication. It is signalling that the emotional agenda in the group is critically important to team health and well- being. It ensures that people can appropriately express and address feelings within the group. It may seem like a big ask of a leader to develop the emotional intelligence skills needed to support the emergence of a high performance team but it is essential. Goleman (2002b) quotes a study by Druskat that shows 'when a team as a whole shows emotional intelligence - that it *resonates* - that predicts that it will be a top performing team, no matter what its performance criteria might be'.

Conflict is surfaced and handled constructively

In such an emotionally mature environment it should be no surprise to learn that HPT members are not frightened to explore and resolve difficult issues without making personal attacks. In many low performing teams conflict is avoided or even repressed but what happens over time in these low performance groups is that conflict left unaddressed will find a way to be heard. It may present as an inappropriate outpouring of anger in front of other colleagues. This is because the team leader lacks the skills or awareness to resolve conflict effectively.

Druskat and Wolff (2001) identify three conditions essential to effective working – 'trust, sense of group identity and sense of group efficacy'. Their research shows 'the most effective teams are emotionally intelligent ones'. Effective groups bring 'emotions deliberately to the surface' to understand 'how they affect the team's work'. The three conditions they identified above are underpinned by the group establishing 'norms for emotional awareness'. This leads to 'true co-operation and collaboration – and high performance overall'. Garvin and Roberto (2001) cite 'constructive conflict' surfacing and resolution as a key requirement of effective decision making in groups. This is conflict which is cognitive rather than affective – focused on the issue or behaviour rather than the person. They go on to describe 'a small set of process traits closely linked with superior outcomes'. These are that effective groups surface multiple alternatives; test assumptions; form well defined criteria (or goals) for decision making; encourage dissent and debate; and pay attention to perceived fairness - described by Ackermann (2005) as 'procedural justice' in groups.

In a HPT the leader will consciously identify and surface points of conflict in order to improve the level of debate and the quality of decision making. The leader will not move on and ignore conflict. Instead it is handled constructively and opposing views are listened to. This does not mean that everyone's opinion shapes the final decision but it does mean that all voices are heard and alternative views considered. Other conflict may be rooted in personality clashes or emotional issues – these too are surfaced and resolved in a safe way.

'Effective groups ... need maintenance' writes Handy (1976) and he explains that this is, in part, focusing on performance and standards but is also about 'encouraging the team, resolving conflict, and promoting listening'. Handy writes that effective teams need to know regularly how they are doing and what their results are. Supremely the leader needs to raise focus on the task 'so that it dwarfs individual needs'. Conflict can derail a team or it can be used to build a team. 'The most challenging risks associated with conflict relate to making it constructive for the team instead of simply enduring it' (Katzenbach and Smith 1993). Polley and Ribbens (1998) argue that 'team wellness needs to be the focus of attention.... so that limiting factors are resolved in ways which are preventative and on-going'. High performance teams deal with both emotional and intellectual conflict.

As one of five children in my family I learned early in childhood that what was required at home was to calm angry situations as soon as possible. I therefore learnt to avoid conflict and felt that I was a 'peace-maker' in the family. I took this learned behaviour into the workplace and my approach to conflict was to try to 'pour oil on troubled waters'. I sought to calm people down before they had opportunity to express the strength of their feelings. In my research into high performance I began to realise that this was unhelpful behaviour and I worked hard to acquire a new skill set which would help me as a leader to work better with the emotional energy in a group. This is a combination of skills including active listening, acknowledging emotions, reflecting back, summarising what was said, showing empathy and seeking resolution. 'Active listening refers to a pattern of listening that keeps you engaged with your conversation partner in a positive way. It is the process of listening attentively while someone else speaks, paraphrasing and reflecting back what is said, and withholding judgment and advice. When you practice active listening, you make the other person feel heard and valued. In this way, active listening is the foundation for any successful conversation' (Cuncic, 2020)

> *'Being heard is so close to being loved that for the average person, they are almost indistinguishable.'*

(Augsburger, 1982)

Much conflict can be resolved simply by listening and hearing the other side. I mean really hearing. Not just letting the other person talk whilst you are planning your next question or response. But deeply listening, letting them express their emotions and thoughts, then reflecting back what they just said so they know you heard it. If you do that, they are going to feel deeply valued - even loved. Simone Weil (from an April 13, 1942 letter) wrote 'attention is the rarest and purest form of generosity'.

✸ ADAPTABILITY

The HPT uses flexible approaches

These groups experiment with new, creative or pragmatic ideas to solve problems. They are also flexible in their approach to time and scheduling.

> *'Productive Hot Spots abound with flexibility.....The challenge for Hot Spots, then, is to reduce as much as possible the negative feelings associated with schedule changes..... One effective way is simply to cultivate the expectation that changes may occur. This becomes a topic of conversation at a relatively early stage and this heedful interaction continues throughout the life span of the Hot Spot.'*

(Gratton, 2007)

The HPT values boundary spanning (new networks)

Within HPT's members are encouraged to hunt for new knowledge outside their familiar or professional networks. This comes from a belief that new knowledge is essential to help the team be creative in the face of challenges and problems. Gratton's (2012) research on high performance groups emphasises the contribution of networking. Gratton found that when professionals network amongst other like professionals what typically happens is a recirculation of 'old knowledge' and communication in their specialised professional language (jargon). However, when professionals start to network amongst unfamiliar professional groupings – for example scientists mixing with musicians – their conversations have the potential to co-create 'new knowledge'. Gratton called this concept boundary spanning and it has significant implications for high performance working. HPTs are able to create and take new knowledge and apply it to products, services and processes to help it achieve its team purpose. New knowledge is used to increase the team's innovation capital and adaptability.

Now discuss the concept with a colleague. What is it telling you? Does your colleague have any insights to offer? Can you identify people in your team who are natural boundary spanners and what can you do to encourage that practice and share the learning from it?

Continuous improvement through reflective learning

HPT's have learning in their DNA profile. Edmondson et al (2001) write that 'the most successful teams had leaders who actively managed the group's learning efforts'. This was based on observations of specialised heart surgery teams faced with radically new procedures.

> 'Complex, subtle issues call for a mind which is working in a slower and altogether less conscious way'

> (Lucas, 2010)

In a HPT, learning from past experience continually shapes future practice. Katzenbach and Smith (1993) found that high performance teams seamlessly integrate their learning and outcomes. They seem to be a visible expression of the learning organisation. Perry (1984) found that 'the implementation of the high performance approach 'involves commitment to learning and risk taking'. In describing team learning in a high performance sports environment, Kernan (2003) writes 'what is special and distinctive about team learning can be seen in the shift from individual to team identity. Successful sports teams describe moments of confluence, peak experiences of intense concentration and awareness when it seems impossible to do wrong'. Kernan goes on, 'this kind of potential opens up in teams when members set aside their personal or departmental agendas and engage emotionally with the team's goals'. Csikszentmihalyi (2002) describes a similar state in *Flow* where athletes, musicians and artists can enter a zone of high performance. He understood that people were at their most productive when they are in a state of what he termed 'flow'.

'The best moments in our lives are not the passive, receptive, relaxing times . . . the best moments usually occur if a person's body or mind is stretched to its limits in a voluntary effort to accomplish something difficult and worthwhile'

(Csikszentmihalyi, 2002)

Oppland (2019) listed eight characteristics of flow:
1. Complete concentration on the task
2. Clarity of goals and reward in mind and immediate feedback
3. Transformation of time (speeding up or slowing down)
4. The experience is intrinsically rewarding
5. Effortlessness and ease
6. There is a balance between challenge and skills
7. Actions and awareness are merged, losing self-con-

scious rumination
8.   There is a feeling of control over the task

When someone is experiencing 'flow' they are immersed in the moment and this is very much a feature of high performance team environments. HPTs are a visible expression of the learning organisation. Perry (1984) found that 'the implementation of the high performance approach 'involves commitment to learning and risk taking'.

Coaching is embedded across the team

Coaching is used in HPT's to reinforce high performance thinking and practice throughout the team. It is not just the leader of the team who uses coaching models and techniques successfully - they are employed across the team regardless of role, position or rank.

Following the introduction of coaching skills into my LSC team they were taken up enthusiastically by all the managers and integrated into performance management conversations with staff. Coaching conversations sprang up everywhere in the office and gradually the culture shifted from simply reviewing achievement against targets to asking powerful questions to stimulate a breakthrough in performance. I knew that this coaching culture had become embedded when I was told that a previously cynical and influential member of staff (who had resisted coaching and other high performance approaches for perhaps a year) had been heard coaching her manager on the office floor in full sight and hearing of colleagues. This told me that not only had coaching become fully accepted by her and that the chief resistor had become a proponent of coaching, but that the manager involved was signalling that coaching was not a 'top down' activity. These were powerful indicators of cultural change.

Many high performing organisations train their leaders in a coaching style of performance improvement. In a coaching programme for Nando's Chicken Restaurants Sir John Whitmore writes of 'transpersonal leadership' helping take organisations into the future – 'bringing together emotional, spiritual and so-cial domains' (Whitmore and Einzig, 2003). Coaches can help people find wider meaning in their work, to explore their voca-tion or mission.

'Everyone has his own specific vocation or mission in life; everyone must carry out a concrete assignment that de-mands fulfillment. Therein he cannot be replaced, nor can his life be repeated. Thus, everyone's task is unique as is his specific opportunity to implement it.'

(Frankl, 2004, first published 1946)

There is a distinction between team building and team learning. Team building addresses 'attitudes and perceptions' whereas team learning raises performance by focusing on issues of Purpose, Pro-cess, Leadership and Context (Kernan, 2003). These help build 'the shared understanding and mental models essential for team per-formance'. Jones et al (1996) have developed at Ashridge College a model for building a high performance team which embeds coach-ing as the primary vehicle for team learning. Their coaching ap-proach encourages the team to develop solutions, indeed the 'team creates everything twice – once in vision, once in reality'. Coaching is such an important part of the leadership and high performance team mix it is given a whole chapter later in this book.

❧ REPUTATION

The HPT leader promotes high performance across organisation
As high performance becomes the new norm in the team its leader starts to carry the high performance message to all who will listen. The leader's enthusiasm for explaining the high performance jour-ney is infectious. They know it works and that it has significant and

sustainable benefits for the organisation, so they want to encourage its wider take-up. They may find that not everyone is interested or that others may even be jealous of the success. However they are not deterred and will find like-minded colleagues who, over a coffee, want to learn more about this cultural transformation.

The reputation of the organisation is improved through the success of the team

The wider enterprise is seen by external stakeholders as getting stronger because of the existence of a single high performance team which is consistently outperforming the expectations of stakeholders. The impact of a HPT is felt beyond the team as external stakeholders start to notice the changes and value them. These stakeholders begin to talk in their own networks about the team. This virtuous circle of success, impact and stakeholder interest is how the HPT'S external reputation is built.

Outsiders notice a positive atmosphere in team

People comment on the great atmosphere they observe in a HPT and are enthused by it. It is impossible to fake such an atmosphere because visitors very quickly sense the true emotional climate in a team or group. They know whether they are welcome, for example, and pick up non-verbal clues as they talk or listen to team members. In the high performance LSC directorate I led we often had visitors from national Head Office who chose to hotdesk amongst us even though they were not meeting colleagues in my Directorate, saying that they preferred the atmosphere of my team to others in the building. These visitors were unaware of our high performance change programme but they felt the welcoming, positive atmosphere and were drawn to it.

Leaders of high performance teams know the importance of laughter in a healthy group. When it is missing they will pay attention to group members' emotional health. When I ran the LSC team I monitored the emotional pulse of the team. When people were 'in the zone' I heard lots of banter, laughter and positive chatter. When things were very quiet, I knew that something was probably wrong. 'A cheerful heart is good medicine', says the Bible (Proverbs 17:22 NIV). Modern science has proved that bible verse. At the Mayo Clinic (2019) they have identified numerous physiological benefits from laughter including:

> '**Short term** - increased take-up of oxygen; released endorphins; our stress response activated and then decreased leaving us 'feeling good'; soothed tension.

> **Long term** – improved immune system by releasing neuropeptides that help fight stress and illness; increased personal satisfaction by helping us connect with others; improved mood, helping to lessen depression and anxiety'.

Laughter acts as an indicator of wellbeing in a team.

✒ LEADERSHIP

The HPT leader's job is to create the conditions in which high performance can emerge. To achieve those conditions leaders need to work on the elements of the high performance model above but there are some specific leadership actions needed.

Leadership is shared across the team

Distributed leadership flows according to the tasks being pursued. Some leaders create dependency and despite their team achieving high results 'they have made themselves indispensable to the effective performance of their group' (Handy, 1976) thereby making the team's results personality dependent and unsustainable. One of the characteristics of high performance teams is that leadership is more likely to be shared. Katzenbach and Smith (1993) explain that the team leader's role in a HPT is less important than might be expected because at some point each team member will step into the leadership role. If a visitor spends some time with a HPT they will find it quite difficult to work out who the team leader is from their observations - it is a fluid use of leadership.

Noble Frankland, former Director of the UK's War Museum, spoke about his wartime experiences in bombers over Germany. He described how leadership moved around the flight crew depending on what was happening:

> *'I never thought I would survive the war.......but I was carried in the arms of a marvellous crew. We acted as one and each of us was the boss at a certain stage of a sortie. On take-off and landing it was the pilot, on the flight to and from the target it was the navigator; over the target it was the bomb aimer; when we were attacked by night fighters it was the rear gunner and the other three who took over'.*

> *(Frankland, Lancaster Navigator 1940-45)*

Schlechty (2001) observed 'Shared leadership... is less like a an orchestra, where the conductor is always in charge, and more like a jazz band, where leadership is passed around ... depending on what the music demands at the moment and who feels most moved to express the music'. Once shared leadership is established it is essential that the leader learns how and when to get out of the way of the team. A HPT is essentially a self-managing team and in terms of achievement of day to day tasks it is perfectly capable of managing without the team leader.

> *'And when you are fortunate enough to spawn a high performance team, get out of its way, and make sure the rest of the organisation is aware of its unique accomplishments and attributes'*

> *(Katzenbach and Smith, 1993)*

This is one of the key points in the high performance journey, when the leadership role changes. If it is properly understood and embraced the HPT leader finds they can safely spend the bulk of their time on external, strategic and reputational activities. Most leaders complain about not having enough time to be able to strategise for example. They say they are constantly fire-fighting urgent issues or problems with difficult staff members, unhappy customers or colleagues. In a HPT environment these time-sapping issues have largely been resolved. The leader is able to reinvent their own role description.

'A leader is best when people barely know that he exists, not so good when people obey and acclaim him, worst when they despise him. Fail to honour people, they fail to honour you. But of a good leader, who talks little, when his work is done, his aims fulfilled, they will all say, "We did this ourselves".'

(Lao Tzu b. 604 BC, Chinese
Philosopher, cited in Shinagel, 2019)

Develops a 'future' mindset with an exciting vision

The leader of the HPT encourages dynamic forward-thinking, with a focus on possibilities. The words they use help people to visualise their shared future as a team. Using Dweck's (2006) terminology the prevailing culture is of a Growth mindset throughout the team. Kotter (1990), writing about the influence of leadership on organisations, sets out three leadership tasks which 'generate highly energised behaviour'. These are direction setting, effective alignment and successful motivation of people. He also describes a leader as' someone who is able to develop and communicate a vision which gives meaning to the work of others'.

Team members feel valued

Everyone's contribution is recognised and HPT leaders catch people doing things right. Leaders go out of their way to reinforce the behaviours they want to see and the positive contributions of team members. If there are failures these are re-framed by the leader as learning opportunities so as to avoid any repetition. Such a culture is the opposite of a blame culture (in which people avoid accountability and innovation) and can be described as a learning culture. It is safe to experiment, within the behavioural values of the team. Jose Mourhino said in an interview in *The Guardian* (2019)

> "Mr Mandela said 'you never lose, you win or you learn'. At United, I won and I learned."

> *(Mourhino, 2019)*

The leader uses metaphor and creates meaning

Symbolic forms and stories are used to powerful effect by the leader. HPT leaders have learned the power of a narrative to envision the team. They will tell personal, true stories about their own vulnerabilities as they seek to increase openness within the team, for example. They will retell compelling stories to inspire action or challenge stereotypical thinking. Deep within our being as humans is a search for meaning. The leaders of HPT's understand this need and ensure the team understands its purpose and comprehends the impact of its work – the 'meaning'. For some this will be expressed in a mission statement, for others it will be understood less prosaically perhaps in terms of the human or economic impact of the work. The leader will make clear what is the difference being made by the work of the team.

> 'Life is not primarily a quest for pleasure, as Freud believed, or a quest for power, as Alfred Adler taught, but a quest for

meaning. *The greatest task for any person is to find meaning in his or her life'*

(Frankl, 2004)

Victor Frankl was a Professor of Neurology and Psychiatry in Vienna who chose not to take up a visa for America in order to look after his ageing parents. He survived four concentration camps including Auschwitz. As a psychiatrist he observed the 'final solution' with different eyes and whilst fully immersed in horror and suffering he was also able to see his experience as a 'living laboratory'. He lived and survived through terrors we can scarcely take in. Frankl concluded that 'those who were oriented towards a meaning to be fulfilled by them in the future were most likely to survive'. This could be a sense of a significant task they had yet to fulfil or a loved person they wanted to be reunited with. In other words they had a deep sense of purpose which gave meaning to their lives despite terrible circumstances. He said the question was not just one of survival but that there had to be a *why* of survival. This was 'a something or a someone' - in other words a focus which was outside the self. Frankl believed that man's primary motivational force is the striving to find meaning in one's own life. He taught that this meaning was not some abstract or general purpose but much closer and immediate. Each person should figure out for their own self what that purpose in life was, but simply chasing success or happiness was missing the point. These things may 'ensue as the unintended side-effects of one's dedication to a cause greater than oneself or as the by-product of one's surrender to a person other than oneself'.

Wise leaders help people find deep meaning in their work. Leaders should use story, metaphor and anecdotes to make clear links between organisational purpose and the inherent worth of work. If people cannot see a higher purpose in their work it will always be just a job. The late John Garnett, Director of the Industrial Society, once told a story of a lady in charge of the tea trolley at the Society. She explained that if she was busy with numerous tea orders it meant that the Society was doing well and people were being trained. She had made a direct link between her daily work, the health of the organisation and the success of those who came for training. As leaders we owe it to our people to discuss and explore what is the greater purpose of our organisations and teams.

Rajan (2004a) is a proponent of the power of conversational metaphor in business and observes that the mark of a high performance organisation is a greater emphasis in day to day conversations on the 'future (the realm of possibility) as opposed to the past (the realm of history) or even the present (the realm of action)'. Bolman and Deal (1997) explore the power of metaphor and symbol in leadership: 'From a symbolic perspective, meaning is the basic human need. Managers who understand symbolic forms and activities and encourage their use help shape an effective organisation'. Leaders of what Bennis (1997) calls Great Groups 'intuitively understand the chemistry of the group...they are able to discern what different people need at different times'. He sets out four behavioural traits of these leaders – they 'provide direction and meaning, generate and sustain trust, display a bias toward action and are purveyors of hope'. One of the enduring characteristics of high performance leaders was revealed in a series of studies undertaken by Bolman and Deal (1991, 1992a, 1992b) who found that 'the ability to use multiple frames was a consistent correlate of effectiveness. Effectiveness as a manager was particularly associated with the structural frame, whereas the symbolic and political frames tended to be the primary determinants of effectiveness as a leader', (Bolman and Deal 1997). Frames are ways of representing reality. They are a way to express meaning. Islamic managers will find it natural to draw on their spiritual knowledge and wisdom to help create meaning in the workplace.

The HPT leader builds team capability

The talents of all are unlocked to build in-depth capacity for both thought and action. Feiner (2002) writes 'high performance leaders see people in terms of their potential and in terms of enabling, teaching and coaching them to meet or exceed that potential'.

'Leaders, like orchestral conductors, are there to enable all the voices or instruments to be heard to their best effect in harmony. Their role as leaders within their specific fields is to identify, develop and use all the talents of their people in a creative symphony of service to the common good'

(Adair, 2018)

Mather (2004), former Chairman of Shell UK, writes 'good leaders motivate individuals and teams by empowering them, and so trusting them to take responsibility for themselves and for the tasks they undertake'. He concluded 'our need is for leadership – those with the purpose, people and passion to set an agenda that will address the long term. Learning from the past, but not living in it'.

Boundaries are managed between team and the organisation

The leader of a HPT builds strong relationships right across their organisation. They become expert at obtaining the resources needed by the HPT and they have an outward-looking leadership style. In a study of 300 self-managing teams, comparing 'average and superior performing' teams, Druskat and Wheeler (2004) found that the leaders of the best performing teams 'excelled at one skill: managing the boundary between the team and the larger organisation'. This process involved influencing the team, having established trust; empowering the team; delegating authority; exercising flexibility regarding team decisions and coaching. Druskat and Wheeler wrote that the leaders of these high performing teams developed 'strong relationships both inside the team and across the organization'.

ꙮ High Performance teams in a Middle East context

In an interview in the Saudi Gazette Randall Peterson (2017a) shared insights from his research on the behaviour of teams in the Middle East. 'Arab Middle Eastern culture is rooted in trust. People are generally guided by tenets of the Quran: they respect their culture, uphold their traditions and value relationships.' Peterson identified five insights into how teams operate in the Middle East.

1. Leaders are shaped by culture – the Middle East is high in 'power distance' often with unequal distribution of power between leaders and followers.

2. Build trust on a foundation of excellence. 'One business leader interviewed as part of Professor Peterson's research said that Islam promoted "sincerity and excellence", which encouraged his team to produce high-quality work'.

3. Everyone has a purpose and a role. An interviewee used this metaphor: "If one part aches because of an ailment, the rest of the body feels the pain. If it weakens from one side, it is strengthened by the other."

4. Open-door culture is common but that doesn't mean that everyone agrees all the time. 'Conflict is inevitable. It's human nature to disagree. If employees suppress their true opinions it "kills the work" declared one leader.

5. Balance consulting with decision-making. Islamic leaders have a religious and ethical imperative to consult before making decisions and they make them in the best interests of the organisation.

Peterson's insights resonate strongly with elements of my high performance team model particularly with regard to:

Adaptability - many teams are multi- cultural and this is potentially a powerful source of strength if harnessed effectively.

Focus and Openness – the moral and religious imperative in Islam to consult before decision-making can be used to reinforce the high performance team's levels of openness and effective communication. Indeed, effective consultation will improve the quality of decision making, reduce conflict and increase the levels of commitment from team members who will feel deeply involved through the process of discussion. The emphasis on trust in working relationships is a great strength along with the focus on excellence. The metaphor of the team being a body is very powerful and indicates the presence of emotional intelligence.

There is an issue to be aware of with leadership. The high power-distance factor in the Middle East has potential to weaken the high performance model and distort feedback. The counter to this is to ensure that pre-decision consultation (shura) is highly effective and that the leader keeps decisions under review so that if new information becomes available an appropriate adjustment can be made. The open door policy will help encourage open communication.

Peterson reflected on the decision making processes he found:

'It's a religious and moral obligation for leaders in the Arab Middle East to consult their people before exercising power. "Consultation is in our Islamic heritage," another leader reminds us. "Even the Prophet Muhammad consulted his companions, taking on their opinions." Though management structures are typically more hierarchical in the Arab Mid-

dle East than in western European firms, decisions taken without consultation are viewed as illegitimate. With that being the case, how are decisions ever made? It seems like a complicated dance. "It's more of an intricate ballet," says Professor Peterson. After consultation with the team, leaders assert their power, making decisions grounded in merit. It's not uncommon to hear managers say, 'I reject an employee's loyalty to me. Loyalty should be to the work alone' or, 'My work is for the sake of the organisation'. Choices are made irrespective of personal opinions; they are made for the good of the organisation. It seems managers in the Arab Middle East make choices based on excellence, so after taking on subordinate's perspectives, their decision stands.'

(Peterson, 2017b)

Summary

The study of high performance teams is essentially a study of groups and how they interact with their leader. High performance can emerge with the right leadership approach and a willingness on the part of the group to realise its full potential. It is clear in Islamic tradition that a leader has to care for and nurture the group they are responsible for. Adair (2010) in *The Leadership of Muhammad* says that a leader is 'there to serve your group or organization, not to impose your greatness upon them but to identify, nurture, draw out and channel their greatness'. Beekun and Badawi (1999) set out a pattern for Islamic leaders which emphasises that:

'Your organization exists to serve Allah; all of its activities should be directed towards that sole purpose as expressed by your vision and mission statements. Transform your organization into one in which learning and tazkiyyah (growth) are an integral part of its culture.'

There can be no greater learning and growth culture that that generated by a high performance team.
It is now time for the reader to complete a diagnostic to assess their chosen team against the elements of the high performance model.

◞ High Performance Diagnostic
This health check tool will help you assess your team against key areas of the high performance model to understand where gaps exist. Circle the level which in your view most closely represents current state. Multiply your circled number by the given weighting multiplier to calculate the weighted score.

Later, ask your team members to give their own ratings.

1	Not in place	2	Understand need	3	Experimenting	4	Embedded practice

FOCUS	Score *(circle)*				Weighting multiplier x	Weighted score
Clear and urgent team purpose- high energy/passion	1	2	3	4	1	
Structure used to team advantage	1	2	3	4	1	
Team develops own measures of success	1	2	3	4	4	
Clear focus on internal customers	1	2	3	4	1	
Clear focus on external customers- exceptional results	1	2	3	4	3	
TOTAL WEIGHTED SCORE						

OPENNESS	Score *(circle)*				Weighting multiplier x	Weighted score
Demanding behaviour standards	1	2	3	4	1	
High levels of trust and commitment to each other	1	2	3	4	2	
There is open communication in the team	1	2	3	4	1	
Emotional intelligence is high within the team	1	2	3	4	5	
Conflict is surfaced and handled constructively	1	2	3	4	1	
TOTAL WEIGHTED SCORE						

ADAPTABILITY	Score *(circle)*				Weighting multiplier x	Weighted score
Team uses flexible approaches	1	2	3	4	1	
Team values boundary spanning (new networks)	1	2	3	4	3	
Continuous improvement through reflective learning	1	2	3	4	3	
Coaching is embedded across the team	1	2	3	4	3	
TOTAL WEIGHTED SCORE						

REPUTATION	Score *(circle)*				Weighting multiplier x	Weighted score
Team leader promotes HP across organisation	1	2	3	4	2	
Reputation of org. improved through success of team	1	2	3	4	5	
Outsiders notice positive atmosphere in team	1	2	3	4	3	
TOTAL WEIGHTED SCORE						

LEADERSHIP	Score *(circle)*				Weighting multiplier x	Weighted score
Leadership is shared across the team	1	2	3	4	3	
Develops 'future' mindset with exciting vision	1	2	3	4	1	
Team members feel valued	1	2	3	4	2	
Leader uses metaphor and creates meaning	1	2	3	4	1	
Leader builds team capability	1	2	3	4	2	
Boundaries managed between team & organisation	1	2	3	4	1	
TOTAL WEIGHTED SCORE						

Create a profile for your team in the box below

Place an X in the box for each total weighted score.
Then join the X's to create a visual profile.

Score	Focus	Openness	Adaptability	Reputation	Leadership	
40						High performance zone
35-39						Real strength - nurture
30-34						Potential strength
25-29						Priority for action
24 or less						Area of concern

DEFINITION OF TERMS

FOCUS	Definitions
Clear and urgent team purpose- high energy/ passion	Team knows why it exists & there is a buzz to its work which people can feel
Structure used to team advantage	Team size is less than 25 members (ideally below 15)
Team develops own measures of success	These are in addition to externally imposed targets
Clear focus on internal customers	Colleagues are treated as customers – expectations managed, needs met

Clear focus on external customers-exceptional results	Team delights in meeting or exceeding agreed outcomes – focus shapes team thinking
OPENNESS	
Demanding behaviour standards	Behaviour norms are high – no passengers carried & team polices own standards
High levels of trust and commitment to each other	Regardless of personal chemistry members have high trust & respect for one another
There is open communication in the team	Honest communication characterises dialogue; reality combined with dignity
Emotional intelligence is high within the team	All members use emotional intelligence to achieve team purpose through effective relationships
Conflict is surfaced and handled constructively	Not frightened to explore & resolve difficult issues - without personal attacks
ADAPTABILITY	
Team uses flexible approaches	Experiments with new, creative or pragmatic ideas to solve problems
Team values boundary spanning (new networks)	Encourages hunt for new knowledge outside familiar networks
Continuous improvement through reflective learning	Learning from past experience continually shapes future practice

Coaching is embedded across the team	Coaching is used to reinforce high performance thinking throughout team
REPUTATION	
Team leader promotes HP across organisation	Carries the high performance message to all who will listen
Reputation of org. improved through success of team	Wider enterprise is seen by external stakeholders as getting stronger
Outsiders notice positive atmosphere in team	People comment on great atmosphere and are enthused by it
LEADERSHIP	
Leadership is shared across the team	Distributed leadership flows according to tasks – leader gets out of way of team
Develops 'future' mindset with exciting vision	Leader encourages dynamic forward-thinking (focus is on possibilities)
Team members feel valued	Everyone's contribution is recognised; leaders catch people doing things right
Leader uses metaphor and creates meaning	Symbolic forms and story used to powerful effect
Leader builds team capability	Talents of all unlocked to build in-depth capacity for thought and action
Boundaries managed between team & organisation	Strong relationships across organisation; resources obtained ; outward-looking leadership

Having completed the diagnostic, ask yourself what will you do to create and sustain high performance? Reflect on the high scores as your areas of strength on which to build. Think about the lower scores as these are the areas for development. Which will you tackle first and why? A great place to start is to ask all team members to complete the diagnostic, summarise the results and then share with the team to encourage a discussion about what they mean.

☙ The key leadership wisdom on the high performance model is:

- High performance covers Focus, Openness, Adaptability, Reputation and Leadership
- Boundary spanning supports high performance
- The zone of high performance is 'Flow'
- Once high performance emerges the leader needs to 'get out of the way'
- High performance teams have the best learning and growth cultures

CHAPTER 9

Practical Leadership wisdom

This chapter contains a treasure chest of practical ideas and approaches which the reader can explore. They may be useful for future reference or to enhance team development which you are already engaged in.

❧ PRACTICAL WISDOM #1:
The sustainability of high performance

> *'Creative energy is sustainable, refuelling itself through the act of creation'*
>
> *(Lucas, 2010)*

Client feedback on the high performance diagnostic prompted me to continue research into the issue of the sustainability of high performance teams and specifically how to avoid individual and team 'burn-out'. The work of Bruch and Vogel (2011) on organisational energy proved to be the missing part of the high performance 'jigsaw'. They defined organisational energy as 'the extent to which an organisation (team) has mobilised its emotional, cognitive and behavioural potential to pursue its goals'. This is very pertinent to the high performance challenge and its sustainability. Bruch & Vogel's research categorised organisational energy into four types.

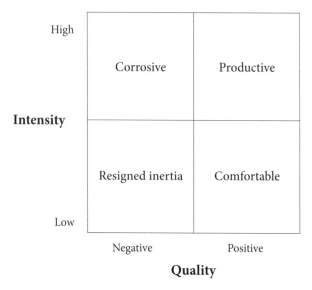

Fig: *Organisational energy (Bruch & Vogel, 2011) adapted*

Bruch & Vogel observed that each of the four organisational energies had particular characteristics:

PRODUCTIVE ENERGY - this is the fuel for high performance and it should be dominant but supported by good levels of Comfortable energy. Productive energy is characterised by emotions, attention & effort mobilised towards achieving common goals; shared alertness; intensely focused work effort and collective enthusiasm.

COMFORTABLE ENERGY – this is the fuel for Productive energy but if it is dominant it leads to complacency, denial & hubris. Comfortable energy is characterised by high satisfaction and being at ease; battery recharging experiences and re-creation e.g. development, creative activity, social events; identification with status quo.

RESIGNED INERTIA – this acts as a deadweight on positive energies. Resigned inertia is characterised by low engagement, indifference to goals; frustration, weakened ability to handle change & innovation; change projects which don't impact behaviour; initiative overload (over-acceleration).

CORROSIVE ENERGY - especially dangerous as it escalates rapidly & destroys trust and value. Corrosive energy is characterised by high levels of anger; dysfunction or distress; low collaboration, busy toxic handlers; harming others (destructive internal conflicts); micro-politics, groups maximising their own interests.

Bruch and Vogel studied organisational energy levels in 187 German companies with 24,000 respondents and their benchmark profile represents the top 10% i.e. high performing companies. The benchmark suggests that Productive Energy levels should be 75 or higher; Comfortable energy levels 70 or higher; and Resigned Inertia and Corrosive levels should be less than 20-25. Organisations in the high performance zone will have an organisational energy profile equal to or better than the German benchmark. In order to maintain high performance, leaders need to invest in maintaining the levels of Productive and Comfortable energies whilst at the same time ensuring that the negative energies are minimised. This is how to make high performance sustainable.

∾❧ PRACTICAL WISDOM #2: **More on leadership styles**
In the leadership development programmes I directed in Middle East settings I noticed that what often worked best were approaches, tools and concepts which supported the four leadership styles identified as having positive impact by Goleman (2000). The four styles shown to have a positive impact on teams and organisations are:

- Authoritative
- Affiliative
- Democratic
- Coaching

Leaders are at their most effective when they are able to use several of these styles appropriately and with integrity. These four styles complement the Leadership Trust leadership definition of 'using our personal power to win the hearts and minds of those around us to achieve a common purpose'. When personal power (which is our leadership influencing energy) is used for positive impact it encourages over time extraordinary levels of commitment and engagement in a team. These four leadership styles are a contributor to high performance and I want to spend some time unpacking the styles.

Our use of any leadership style is an expression of our belief about leadership and power. Personal power can be used negatively to compel others to do something we want them to do – but this approach has a negative impact on the team and is to be avoided. The first negative style is **Pacesetting** which seeks to get fast results but it needs to have in place a highly motivated, competent team. Such a leader sets very high personal standards for performance and demonstrates these by personal example. However, others can feel overwhelmed and resentful when a pacesetting leader shows intolerance of mistakes and actually takes over the work. They are exhausting to be around. Pacesetting leaders show conscientiousness, a strong drive to achieve and often take the initiative.

The second negative style is **coercive leadership** which may have some advantages in a short term crisis or when working with certain problem employees who will not cooperate but it has hugely negative outcomes for team and organisational culture. Leaders who choose this style will demonstrate self-control, a strong drive to achieve and will often take the initiative. However, this 'do what I tell you' style brooks no argument, questioning or debate. It will threaten people with punishments if they dis-obey. There is also some doubt about how effective it actually is in situations which are fast moving and chaotic – as shown in the following case study on sense-making in difficult times:

'Paul Gleason is acknowledged as one of the best wildland fire-fighters in the world, and his take on leading has led to the service employing a simple protocol that fire chiefs use to give direction to crews in the middle of a fire-fight. It involves many conversations along the lines of....

"Here's what I think we face; here's what I think we should do, and why; here's what we should keep our eye on. Now talk to me.....tell me if you do not understand, or cannot do it. What are you thinking that I may have missed? Tell me if you see something that I do not see."

What happens next emerges from the conversation, but it is not a plan or strategy for the whole job. Gleason prefers to see his leadership efforts as a continuous process of sense-making, rather than decision-making. This gives his crew a direction for some indefinite period which is dynamic, open to revision at any time, responsive, self-correcting and with more of its rationale being transparent. Gleason says, "If I make a decision it is a possession, I take pride in it, I tend to defend it and not listen to those who question it. If I 'make-sense' then this is more dynamic and I listen and I can change it. You can't be threatened by people wanting to know - you're a leader not a wizard"

This approach:
- Encourages Updating
- Facilitates respectful interaction
- Animates People
- Generates Direction

Perhaps these open processes of engagement have something helpful to say in other workplaces?'

(Weick, 2002) abridged

We can conclude that the pace setting and coercive leadership styles are generally best avoided. We will now look at the four positive styles which Goleman's research has shown work best especially when two or more are combined in an integrative approach to leadership.

The **authoritative style** has the most positive impact overall. This 'come with me' approach states the overall goal for a team or organisation but gives people in the team flexibility to choose how they achieve it. So it is very clear on what needs to be done but very flexible on how it is achieved. This approach has positive impacts because it places power in the hands of team members – this increases ownership of the outcomes. Employee motivation and discretionary effort increase; people choose to give more, make more effort, go the 'extra mile' to get their work done. The authoritative style works best where clear direction is needed on aims. However a word of warning here – do not use it when leading a team of experts as it risks being seen as overbearing. Leaders who choose this style draw on the emotional intelligence strengths of self-confidence and empathy. They work as a change agent.

The **affiliative style** seeks to put people first. It creates harmony and builds strong emotional bonds between people. It is very appropriate to use in a team which has experienced relationship fractures or has low morale. It seeks to improve communication, build trust, share ideas, increase flexibility, encourage innovation and develop loyalty. It has some down-sides however in that, because it is low on the giving of advice, some people may be left guessing as to what exactly is required to be done. Also the affiliative style can over use praise which can lead to an inappropriate acceptance of underperformance. The affiliative style leader uses the emotional intelligence areas of empathy, building relationships and communication. The style has a positive impact but is best combined with Authoritative to give direction first followed by nurturing.

The **democratic style** seeks to forge consensus through participation. The leader asks 'What do you think?' in order to build buy-in and commitment from employees. It can be a useful style to use one to one or in small groups to get input and feedback from valued team members. It can help to build organisational flexibility and responsibility as it gives people space and time to debate issues and analyse problems together. However if overused it can create a culture of endless meetings which may leave people feeling confused or even frustrated if no action is seen to be happening. In this overuse scenario, organisational energy is being drained away in 'paralysis by analysis'. Democratic style leaders use the emotional intelligence strengths of collaboration, team leadership and communication.

The **coaching style** is the fourth style to have positive impact. It seeks to use powerful questions to elicit answers from team members. It is essentially a search for wisdom. It asks 'What else?' in order to help create reflective space for colleagues who probably know the answers to issues but do not realise that they know. It is highly developmental as it increases people's capacity to problem solve and experiment with solutions and feelings. It helps employees and teams improve long term performance and strengths. It works best with people who want to grow and develop. Using this style needs the leader to acquire coaching skills so that their questioning does not become intrusive or directive. Coaching needs to be given time to produce results because it is dependent on the coachee's learning cycle. The coaching style leader uses emotional intelligence strengths of developing others, empathy and self-awareness.

☙ PRACTICAL WISDOM #3: **A mindset that works**

Dweck's (2006) work on mindset began in classrooms of children and young people. She was interested to understand why some young people were avid learners with strong resilience to failure and why others gave up when faced with difficulties and initially low results. You may want to complete a mindset diagnostic to gain some insights into your own preferences. Diehl (2008) has a useful one on the internet - see the reference section. Dweck found that some people showed a Fixed mindset whilst others approach learning with a Growth mindset.

The Fixed mindset believed that intelligence was static. These folk wanted to look smart and had a tendency to avoid challenges, become defensive, give up easily, saw effort as fruitless and ignored useful feedback which they saw as negative. They felt threatened by the success of others. Fixed mindset leads people to reach a performance plateau early in life and they achieve less than their full potential. They want success without having to make much effort in their learning. The Fixed mindset says I want to look intelligent at all costs. They feel success should come naturally. They hide mistakes, conceal deficiencies, give up, retreat to their comfort zone, blame others or try to feel superior.

Fixed mindset people say things like:

"When I do my work I want to show how good I am at it".
"When I work hard…..it makes me feel I am not very smart".
"I would try not to take this subject ever again".

On the contrary Growth mindset people believe that intelligence can be developed. They believe intelligence is not static or fixed. They show a strong desire to learn and a tendency to embrace challenge, persist in the face of setbacks, see effort as the path to mastery, learn from criticism and feedback and find lessons and inspiration in the stories and successes of others. They progress to ever higher levels of achievement and feel that talent is a starting point not the end of a journey. The Growth mindset says learn, learn, learn. This mindset believes that working hard and making effort are keys to success. They believe that you should capitalise on mistakes and confront deficiencies.

Growth mindset people say things like:

"It's much more important for me to learn things than it is for me to get the best grades".
"The harder you work at something, the better you get at it".
"I will work harder on this".

Dweck (2006) showed that mindsets come from the values of parents, teachers and bosses and that it was words which revealed their values.

Praising *intelligence* encouraged a fixed mindset, for example "That's a really good result. You must be good at this".

Praising *effort* encouraged a growth mindset, for example "That's a really good result. You must have tried really hard".

As a leader we need to use words which encourage a growth mindset in others. We should praise effort, struggle, strategies, choices, choosing difficult tasks, learning, improving and persistence in the face of setbacks. The leader should portray skills as acquirable; value passion, effort and improvement over natural talent; and encourage self-mentoring rather than self-judging.

Dweck (2006) showed that mindset can be changed because it is a learned and habitual response to stimuli. The brain gets stronger the more it is used, in the same way as our muscles. We can literally 'change our mind'. This has important implications for the leader in their choice of language, what to focus on, and the culture they seek to create in an organisation or team. Dweck (2006) wrote, 'Members of growth-mindset groups are more likely to state their honest opinion & openly express disagreements' and 'only people with a growth mindset pay close attention to information that could stretch their knowledge'. It is the leader's role to create the right conditions in which people can grow and develop to achieve their full potential. Growth mindset is a powerful leadership tool in this cause.

❧ PRACTICAL WISDOM # 4: **Motivation**

Pink (2010) explored the science of motivation and found that using incentives or punishments (what he called 'carrots and sticks') does not work except for tasks requiring minimal cognitive skill. He found that carrots and sticks extinguish intrinsic motivation, diminish performance and crush creativity. They have a tendency to crowd out good behaviour, encourage cheating, shortcuts and unethical behaviour. He also found that they become addictive and foster short term thinking.

Once people feel they are being paid fairly, then intrinsic motivators are much more powerful. Pink listed these as a desire for autonomy, mastery and purpose in their work. Autonomy is about giving employees space for self-direction wherever possible. Mastery is the desire to continually improve at something which matters. Pink describes purpose as the desire to do things in service of something larger than ourselves. You can watch a video of Pink expanding these ideas – see the Useful Resources section.

❧ PRACTICAL WISDOM # 5: **Great work**

Bungay Stanier (2010, 2016) is passionate about leaders creating workplaces in which great work can flourish. In my Useful Resources section you will find a link to the excellent short animation Stanier has produced to explain Great Work.

Great Work could be defined as work which makes a real

difference in the lives of our stakeholders

Bad Work could be what gets in the way of that

Good (Busy) Work is all the other stuff

Take three pieces of paper and make one list for your Great Work, one list for your Good Work and one list for your Bad Work. *Be specific.* This is going to inform your next steps. Once you have done that find a like-minded and trusted colleague at work and discuss and identify how you will

- increase Great Work
- stop doing the Bad Work.

Remember to listen! Be curious. Build on the ideas shared.
Doing this review is not easy and it needs focus, courage and resilience. The challenge now is for you to find a way to put your analysis into action.

☙ PRACTICAL WISDOM # 6: **Common dysfunctions of a team**
This insight is for when it is all going wrong in a team and you want to understand what is happening. Lencioni (2005) showed that a strong and healthy team is effective on five elements.

When these are not going well Lencioni described them as the five dysfunctions.

Higher trust

Trust works primarily on an emotional level. When trust is present it means it's OK to be vulnerable with each other and you can be open with other team members. Communication is without filters.

Resolving conflict

Trusting teams are not afraid to have difficult conversations. They address issues and decisions which are keys for organisational success. They will disagree, challenge and question in order to find the best answers and make great decisions.

Higher commitment

As trust grows in the team, and the quality of conversations improves with unfiltered conflict, then commitment rises. The team achieves real buy-in even when team members have initially disagreed with one another. All opinions and ideas are heard which gives confidence that no stone is unturned.

Embracing accountability

Teams that commit like this do not hesitate to hold each other accountable. They don't rely on the team leader as the primary source of accountability but go directly to their colleagues because it matters.

Focus on results

Teams that trust each other, engage in productive conflict, commit to decisions and hold each other accountable will set aside personal agendas, egos and departmental game-playing. They focus exclusively on what is best for the team and organisation. Collective results define team success.

It is interesting to compare the work of Maslow (see page 93) and Lencioni. The 'self-actualisation' principle applies in both models with individual needs being successively met in Maslow's approach and team needs being met in Lencioni's.

❧ Key wisdom from this chapter is:
- High performance can become sustainable with the right organisational energies
- Leadership styles which best support high performance are Authoritative, Affiliative, Democratic and Coaching
- High performance needs a Growth mindset
- Intrinsic motivators are the most powerful (autonomy, mastery and purpose)
- Increase the Great Work and stop the Bad Work
- Strong and healthy teams will achieve outstanding results

CHAPTER 10

Leadership wisdom for coaching

The Prophet said, "Facilitate things to people (concerning religious matters), and do not make it hard for them and give them good tidings and do not make them run away (from Islam)."

(Narrated by Anas bin Malik: Sahih al-Bukhari, Vol. 1, Book of Knowledge, Hadith 69)

We saw earlier how the 'coaching' style of leadership has been associated with higher levels of performance. This chapter looks at the nature and practice of coaching and introduces a model suitable for the manager who wants to acquire coaching skills for the first time. It also introduces a more advanced model for those familiar with the foundations of coaching, which focuses on solutions thinking.

What is coaching?

The person leading the coaching session is the 'coach'. The person who is being coached is the 'coachee'. Coaching is a structured process to help a coachee achieve their goals. Cleary (1995) defined a key goal of coaching was to improve work results by increasing an employees' capability for managing their own performance.

'Coaching is also an open ended process which analyses the present situation, defines the performance goals, elicits per-

*sonal and extra-personal resources and implements a plan
to achieve the goal'*

(King & Eaton, 1999)

A coaching conversation starts from the present situation and
is rooted in what is actually happening at work. It aims to achieve
set outcomes via action planning. It is up to the coachee to identify the issue to tackle in each coaching session. Whitmore, quoting
Gallwey (1986), writes 'coaching is unlocking a person's potential
to maximise their own performance. It is helping them to learn
rather than teaching them'. The coach's role is to facilitate accelerated learning in the person being coached.

*'Put simply, coaching is a conversation, or a series of conver-
sations, one person has with another. The person who is the
coach intends to produce a conversation that will benefit the
other person, the coachee, in a way that relates to the coachee's
learning and progress. Coaching conversations might happen
in many different ways and in many differing environments'*

(Starr, 2003)

What are the benefits of coaching?
Coaching is about helping others to make personal change. It is
also about enabling organisational change. These two things are
often inter-related. When coaching is practised well it has numerous benefits which includes:

THE COACH (assuming he/she is a line manager)
- Improves managerial and interpersonal skills
- Acquires new skills and abilities
- Increases self-awareness
- Gains new perspectives on work issues

- Effective coaching releases more time for other things (less time is spent 'managing' employees)
- Reduces stress
- Helps achieves the task, build the team and develop individuals
- Builds trust and openness
- Supports the learning team

THE COACHEE

- Develops increased adaptability to change
- Learns to solve their own problems and how to unlock barriers at work
- Has a positive impact on performance
- Releases discretionary effort
- Increases motivation and capability
- Helps them be more effective through transitions and change
- Helps them experiment with new skills, behaviours or thinking
- Stimulates creative problem solving
- Increases emotional intelligence through awareness

Coaching helps people access and explore the way they see their world at work. It helps them develop clear goals and intentions. It is essentially a learning (reflective) conversation. It has great power because it engages the imagination. It seeks out bridging solutions and work-arounds. It pays attention to the emotional agenda at work – to people's feelings. Coaching is about considering possibilities.

It has been said that 'coaching creates things twice – first in the imagination and then in practice'.

'...all things are created twice. There is a mental (first) creation, and a physical (second) creation. The physical creation

follows the mental, just as a building follows a blueprint. If you don't make a conscious effort to visualize who you are and what you want in life, then you empower other people and circumstances to shape you and your life by default. It's about connecting again with your own uniqueness and then defining the personal, moral, and ethical guidelines within which you can most happily express and fulfill yourself. '

(Covey, 2020)

Coaching is not an opportunity for the coach to be directive, which would be a serious abuse of the coaching process and must be avoided. It is not a cosy chat about work over a cup of tea. Coaching is person-centred but always goal - directed. Coaching is never a substitute for personal therapy or counselling because these needs must be met by a qualified and experienced therapist not by a coach. Neither is it an appraisal session in which the coach returns to their managerial role and acts as the line manager reviewing performance. It is not an opportunity for a hidden agenda to be followed by the coach perhaps by manipulating an outcome or approach.

Coaching approach and behaviours
It is the coach who is responsible for managing the coaching process. The coach should aim to help the coachee reflect on what they are noticing. It is important to take time in each session to build rapport with the coachee as this will build the coaching relationship. The coach should help put the coachee at ease and show genuine interest in the situation. Whichever coaching model you choose to use remember not to rush the coaching cycle or process. Give the coachee plenty of time to think about their answers to your questions - a good coach is happy to work with the silences. The coach should avoid telling the coachee what to do or think. The coach should encourage the coachee to generate ideas and under-

take analysis of their issue. What works best is that the coach believes the coachee knows the answer already – even though it may
need several sessions to get there. Coaches need an underpinning
belief or philosophy that people can learn and change.

The hardest thing for a coach to do is stay silent when you
know the answer but the coachee has not yet figured out the
solution. Coaches should avoid offering solutions unless the coachee is completely stuck and no amount of skilled questioning
can bring out what is not there. In that case the coach might ask
'Would you like me to suggest a solution?' but if that offer is accepted the coach must quickly switch back to coaching mode after offering the solution.

The coach engages with a coachee's mental maps and metaphors to help them reflect and make sense of their thinking about
action at work.

> *'What is a metaphor? Simply put, a metaphor is a figure
> of speech containing an implied comparison. With meta-
> phors, words or phrases that are ordinarily applied to one
> thing are applied to something you wouldn't necessarily
> pair it with.*
>
> *Here's a metaphor example: "The curtain of night fell upon
> us." In this metaphor, the evening did not develop into a vel-
> vet curtain. Rather, simple words are being used to paint a
> colorful picture. Now, we know it is nighttime, but it's been
> written in a manner that alludes to how quickly night ar-
> rived with the kind of darkness that comes from closing a
> thick curtain.'*

> *(Yourdictionary, 2019)*

Coaching conversations should be confidential so that trust
is built between the coach and coachee. The usual boundaries

around harm apply though – the coach should intervene if they believe there is a risk of significant harm to the coachee or other people. That situation will be very rare indeed.

The skills needed by the coach
- Use open questions (sensitively probe when needed) which need more than a yes/no answer
- Actively listen
- *How* are things being said?
- Develop your emotional intelligence – be aware of the coachee's emotions and body language
- Check out assumptions and meanings
- Listen for the metaphors and themes used by the coachee
- What is the emerging story?
- Reflect back in summary form what you hear being said ('so what you are saying is…')
- Keep the coachee focussed on the issue
- If you need to challenge, do so with and support and respect
- Treat the coachee with dignity – they make their own decisions
- Afterwards, reflect on your own coaching approach – what worked well and why; what did not work well and why. Some coaches use a supervisor to help with this process.

❧ A Foundational Model Of Coaching - GROW.
The GROW model, when used properly by the coach, raises awareness in the coachee along with an increased sense of responsibility. The coachee focuses their attention on a work issue they choose and through the coaching process takes responsibility for their thoughts and actions. Within that context the coach helps the coachee walk through a simple framework by their use of helpful questions covering four areas.

GOAL
REALITY
OPTIONS
WILL

GROW has been used by coaches across the world to help increase the self-motivation of coachees. It is simple, straightforward and it works. The more a coach uses the framework and the suggested questions, the more confident they will become in the practice. I used the GROW model throughout the DQP/HQP programmes in Iraq and it was well received and quickly learned. Pilot group participants underwent coaching on the first programme and were then trained to carry out the coaching themselves in subsequent programmes. The advantages of this were that Iraqi coaches were already fluent in cultural sensitivities which may have been missed by Western coaches; coaching could take place without the need to translate; it built sustainability helping Iraqi coaches maintain the programme benefits in subsequent years.

Eaton and Johnson's (2001) little book *Coaching Successfully* is one of the most accessible available for those new to coaching and they write:

> 'coaching is the art of improving the performance of others. Managers who coach encourage their teams to learn from and be challenged by their work. Create the conditions for continuous development by helping your staff to define and achieve goals'.

The coaching style is one of the most effective leadership styles available and it can be used both in formal coaching sessions and just as effectively informally. A manager can 'walk and coach' by using a few well-placed questions, for example. A telephone conversation can be turned into a short coaching session at almost

any point. It is perfectly possible to use coaching questions upwards to your line manager once you have some experience of
using coaching questions. The power of a coaching question is
that it elicits learning in the person being asked the question.

ᴄᴏ The GROW framework

The coach follows a four step process by asking questions of the
coachee which cover the GROW cycle. The stages can be used
flexibly - for example many coachees will naturally move into
discussing the current Reality as a first step as they may not be
ready to articulate their Goal. The framework is not meant to be
a constraint but it gives a useful structure for the coach to follow.

Here are some suggested questions which may be helpful to
get you started or to be used as an aide-memoire. Feel free to
phrase them in your own words.

GOAL **questions might include:**
- What would you like to talk about in this coaching ses-
  sion today?
- What do you want to achieve in this session today?
- What is your longer term goal in relation to this work issue?
- How will you know when you have achieved that goal
  (what will success look like)?

REALITY **questions might include:**
Thinking about the work issue you have chosen
- What is the background story?
- What is happening at work right now?
- What actions have you already taken concerning this and
  what did you learn from that?
- What is stopping you go forward on this issue?
- Is there anything else going on (intuition)?
- Has anyone else solved this problem before? What does
  that tell you?

- What resources do you have for this change? What do you need?

OPTIONS questions might include:
- What could you do as your next step?
- What else?
- Is there another option?
- What are the benefits/costs of each option?
- *What if* you had more…..time/money/power etc?
- *What if* there were no history or politics – what could you do?
- What would happen if you did nothing?

WILL questions might include:
- Which option(s) do you choose?
- Will this meet your goal?
- How will you know you have been successful?
- When will you start and finish?
- What could hinder you?
- What support do you need?
- How will you enlist that support?
- On a 1 -10 scale (with 1 as low and 10 as high) what commitment do you have to taking action?
- What will move this commitment up one point?
- Then summarise the action the coachee has committed to

Adapted from Whitmore (2002)

A coaching session is typically about 60 - 90 minutes (more than that may tire the coachee) and sessions no more frequent than monthly to allow time for the coachee to take action and to reflect. Coaching for most people works best face to face, because this allows the coach to read body language more easily, though circumstances such as Covid-19 restrictions or geographical distance may dictate it takes place on the phone or in a video call.

However it is done both parties need to ensure the session is free of distractions and any interruptions. It should be a high quality, protected conversation.

Coaches should aim to be 'good enough' rather than perfect in their coaching. You will make mistakes especially in the first few coaching sessions as you gain experience. The coach needs to be committed to their own learning as a coach and they should encourage feedback from the coachee as to how the coaching process is going. This will give additional real-time data to the coach on the impact of coaching. Every coachee is different so the coach needs to be prepared to treat each new coachee as a unique person with unique challenges.

❧ A more advanced coaching model: Solutions Focused coaching

A 'solutions focus' to coaching is a model which brings the practice of coaching into an entirely different space. Jackson & McKergow (2002) write:

> 'With this approach you will sidestep the often fruitless search for the causes of problems, take the direct route forwards and simply head straight for the solution. The focus on solutions (not problems), the future (not the past) and what's going well (rather than what's gone wrong) leads to a positive and pragmatic way of making progress.'

Jackson & McKergow's approach is grounded in three solutions focused principles:

- 'Don't fix what isn't broken
- Once you know what works – do more of it
- It it's not working, do something different'

It needs talk about solutions (which are the realm of possibilities) not talk about problems (which are all about the causes of problems). The GROW model has a tendency to focus the coachee on barriers and problems to be overcome and for some people this may prove unhelpful as it can be biased towards the past. The Solutions Focus arguably has a stronger bias towards the future.

'Problem Talk' includes questions like
- What's wrong with what you are doing?
- Why are things doing badly?
- What's the main cause of your difficulty?
- Whose fault is it?
- What else makes it a problem?

'Solutions Talk' uses very different questions
- What are you aiming to achieve?
- How will you know you've achieved it?
- What was the best you ever did (at this thing)?
- What went well on that occasion?
- What will be the first signs that you're getting better?
- How will other people notice improvement?

Solutions Focused coaching pays close attention to the desired results and the nature of the coaching conversation which is needed. It seeks to take a direct route to the solution. Jackson and McKergow (2002) maintain that the choice of language used by the coach is important as it brings influence upon planned action. People may use the phrase 'talk me through the problem' but Solutions Focus wants to be walked through the answer.

'Things should be made as simple as possible, but no simpler'

(Attributed to Albert Einstein by Sessions, 1950)

The solutions focused coaching model (Jackson & McKergow, 2002) uses 'OSKAR' as a key part of its approach: Outcomes, Scale, Know-how, Affirm/Action, and Review.

Outcomes – jointly define the coaching outcome
Scale –from 1 to 10
Know How – knowledge, skills, resources, attributes
Affirm – compliment skills & resources with Action – decide next small steps
Review – what's better? what helped? what's next?

Outcomes

At the start of the coaching conversation, ask the coachee to define the coaching outcome. Ask them what is their objective and what they want to achieve. Then ask them to describe their *perfect future* for the issue to be addressed. This is a question which can strongly engage their imagination. You are asking them to imagine that whilst they were asleep a miracle happened and their big work problem vanished! What will be the first signs, as they walk into work, which tell them it has happened? What would they notice? What would others notice? Don't rush this opening part of the conversation. You are effectively immersing the coachee in the solution as they visualise it in their head. They may want to talk about how it would feel or sound. What they are describing to you is shaping their ultimate goal. You will often see an emotional engagement in the coachee as they allow their imagination to work. Watch their body language.

Scaling

Now ask the coachee to use the scaling tool. You ask them to use a scale of 1 to 10 (where 1 is the worst and 10 represents the perfect future) to score their issue today against their perfect future. They will speak out a number (X). As a coach you may think they have scored too low or too high but everyone's scale is right for them. Don't interfere. The next question is about the first small step they can take to start creating their perfect future. Ask them 'What would get you to X +1?'

Know how

You now need to help the coachee explore what resources they have to help create the perfect future. This might include knowledge, skills, resources or attributes. The coach should ask about the 'things that count' - the relevant know-how. Start with asking what got them to X already and what helped get them there. When does the outcome they want happen already – even a small amount? Explore their answers with follow up questions including how did parts of the perfect future start emerging? Where else is this happening? Who else can help? It is good to work with the silences in conversations and a great follow up question is "what else?" Then wait. These questions are designed to draw out 'Solutions Talk'.

Affirm

Having helped the coachee identify the small steps being taken already which are moving them towards the perfect future and the resources and know-how they have, the next task is to compliment that know-how. This is about affirming or praising what's already going well. This will help build their confidence.

Action

A key premise of Solutions Focus is doing more of what works. It is this which is most likely to succeed and is probably the easiest action to prioritise. You are asking the coachee to notice what works already. If something isn't working then the coachee needs to identify what needs to stop. Ask the coachee to choose things to do tomorrow which are concrete.

Remember, ask them to:
- *Do more of what works*
- *Stop doing what isn't working*

Review

The review would be done at the start of the next session because it is a review of action, impact and learning. The coachee needs to go away and start moving towards their perfect future. In the review don't focus on barriers but rather what is working and how. Jackson and McKergow (2002) write 'as a coach, part of your role is to assist performers to take the credit (or at least a part of it) for their successes'. Help build their confidence.

☙ Aide Memoire for coaching

Oskar coaching questions might include:

Outcomes – define the coaching outcome *The vision of the future*
• What is the objective for this coaching session? • What do you want to achieve? • What is your Perfect Future?
Scale – from 1 to 10   Setting the baseline
• On a scale of 1 to 10 (10 = Perfect Future) what would you score your issue today on how near it is to 10? • What would it take for you to get to x+1? The coach can ask them to scale for confidence, commitment to act etc.
Know How – knowledge, skills, resources, attributes *Ask about the things that count – relevant know-how*

- What got you to x already?
- What helps you perform at that level?
- What attributes help you achieve that?
- When does the outcome you want happen already – even a small amount?
- Where else is this happening?
- Who can help you?

Affirm – compliment skills & resources
Encourages a resourceful state
Action – decide next small steps
Doing more of what works

- What are you noticing that works already?
- Can you stop doing what isn't working?
- What **action** is most likely to succeed?
- What are the next small steps?
- Scale for confidence to take action….
- What will raise that confidence +1?

Review – of action, impact and learning

- What's happening? What's better?
- What helped?
- What did you do to make that happen? What did others do?
- What impact has it had?
- Who noticed?
- What have you learned?
- What will change next?

Adapted Jackson and Waldman (2006) unpublished course '*Advanced Coaching with the Solutions Focus*' for CEL

❧ Other powerful coaching questions to build your coaching habit

Michael Bungay Stanier is an award-winning Canadian coach who is concerned with transforming the way we work. Bungay Stanier (2016) recommends seven powerful questions in our coaching practice. You can add them into your portfolio as you gain experience.

1. The **Kickstart** question to focus and open
   - *What's on your mind?*

2. The **Awe** question to boost things
   - *And what else?*

3. The **Focus** question to get to the heart of the challenge
   - *What's the real challenge here for you?*

4. The **Foundation** question to also get to the heart of the challenge
   - *What do you want?*

5. The **Lazy** question which will save you hours
   - *How can I help?*

6. The **Strategic** question which will save time for those you ask it
   - *If you are saying yes to this, what are you saying no to?*

7. The **Learning** question helps to bookend things
   - *What was most useful for you?*

These are questions to use if you are finding you get stuck from time to time as you coach others. Use them flexibly and see what impact you notice. There are more resources from Bungay Stanier in the Useful Resources section of this book.

❧ Key wisdom from this chapter on coaching for high performance is:

- The coaching style of leadership is associated with higher levels of performance
- Coaching creates things twice – first in the imagination and then in practice
- Coaches help people make sense of their thinking about work
- A foundational coaching model is GROW - a great place to start
- A more advanced model is OSKAR - solutions focused coaching
- Collect your own set of powerful coaching questions based on what works well for you
- Keep building your coaching skills

CHAPTER 11

Leadership wisdom for change

'And we made them leaders guiding men by our command and We sent inspiration to do good deeds, to establish regular prayers, and to practice regular charity; and they constantly served Us only'

(Qur'an, 21:73).

Good deeds of 'change' may be needed at the individual, team or organisational level. Change will certainly be needed within the leader himself as he (or she) grapples with the challenges of leadership. Reinhold Niebuhr is attributed by *Qouteinvestigator*, (2020) with the prayer that God would:

'Grant me the serenity to accept the things I cannot change; courage to change the things I can; and wisdom to know the difference'.

There is no point striving against things totally outside our control. There is every point in giving all our energy to change the things we can indeed influence. Niebuhr is saying that the wise leader can tell the difference between these two positions.

A leader can only be effective if they are able to lead change well. To do this requires being able to engage your people in the purpose and meaning of the change. Remember the Leadership Trust's wisdom that leadership is 'Using our personal power to *win the hearts and minds* of those around us to achieve a common purpose'. Leading change is fundamentally about winning hearts and minds. It is about having a sound logic and methodology for the change project but it is even more about having a compelling emotional logic. Adair (2010) writes 'any plan is bad that is not susceptible to change'.

Beekun and Badawi (2009) wrote 'there can be no leader without followers, and no followers without a leader... (so) a leader must remember that he cannot force others to change'. Leadership is a highly relational phenomenon and wise leaders are aware of that and work with the dynamics in the room. Unwise leaders are not aware of this truth and remain oblivious to the emotional wake they leave behind them as they seek to make changes.

Evidence shows again and again that most transformational change projects fail, indeed about 70% of them fail on their own terms (Hartley, 2002). This means that these projects did not achieve the objectives they were targeted with. They did not create the return on investment which was promised. This is a huge waste of resources. Why do they fail? It is typically not because of poor project management methodologies but much more to do with a failure to engage the people affected by the change. If change is imposed without a compelling and complete rational *and* emotional logic it will probably fail because the stakeholders and actors involved have not 'bought in'. They become at best observers and at worst destructive saboteurs. What many people describe as resistance to change is in fact resistance to the bad leadership of change; it is resistance to unwise leadership.

'You are braver than you believe, stronger than you seem, and smarter than you think.'

(Attributed to A.A.Milne, but actually an anonymous Disney writer)

Leadership takes courage, strength and wisdom and you may have more of those resources than you think. This chapter aims to add to your stock of wisdom in order to lead change more effectively. It introduces 'The Change House' - an approach which we shared with Iraqi leaders. They found that it proved effective in helping them understand reactions to change in their institutions and how to navigate them. There was considerable amusement when the model was introduced and we did not understand the reason for the laughter until it was explained that 'change my house' in Iraq means to change your wife. We were not proposing to change anyone's wife!

Organisations are not machines - they are living, dynamic organisms made up of a network of human relationships. When a leader seeks to make a change in an organisation it inevitably means that relationships will need to change. Changing relationships is not like changing a tyre or fixing a mechanical problem. Changing relationships requires a willingness to change, a willingness to be influenced, a sense of openness and a sense of reciprocity. If a leader assumes agreement for change is high when it is in fact low, and the degree of certainty about the change is low, they may unintentionally move the team or organisation into chaos. They are then left wondering 'what just happened?' and may seek to blame others for their own mistaken and unhelpful approach to change. Effective leadership of change requires high levels of skill, emotional intelligence, courage, reflexivity and adaptability. It represents one of the greatest challenges for a leader.

'Most textbooks focus heavily on techniques and procedures for long-term planning, on the needs for visions and missions, on the importance and the means of securing strongly shared cultures, on the equation of success with consensus, consistency, uniformity and order. [However, in complex environments] the real management task is that of coping with and even using unpredictability, clashing counter-cultures,

disensus, contention, conflict, and inconsistency. In short the task that justifies the existence of all managers has to do with instability, irregularity, difference and disorder.'

Stacey (1996)

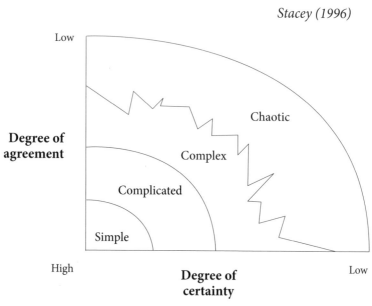

Illustration of Stacey from JISC (2019)

The figure shows the approach toward chaos, as agreement lessens and certainty weakens. Ordinary management skills are appropriate for when certainty and agreement are high but it takes wise and extraordinary leadership to steer an organisation which finds itself near the edge of chaos. A Dean once described Iraq to me as a 'chaos country' which teeters on the edge of uncertainty. It seems that the leadership of change could be improved.

✒ The Change House

Janssen (1996) first developed the concept of 'The Four Rooms of Change' but over time others including Ashridge Consulting (adapted by Smallwood) added to the concept and the model used on the DQP and HQP programmes is the one shared in this book. It draws on the thinking of Stacey, Griffin & Shaw (2000), Kubler-Ross's (1969) work on bereavement responses and transitions as well as Schein's work (2010) on organizational culture. The Change House gives the leader a framework in which to assess and then influence the states of mind which impact change. The model can be applied to individuals, teams or organisations. There are several phases of change and each has their own emotional dynamics. The models helps a leader think about people's readiness and levels of energy for change. It helps the leader think about how constructively to move people on from each of the four rooms.

Movement through the Change House needs to be anticlockwise from room to room as shown in the illustration. People do not have to spend the same amount of time in each room - it is possible to move through some rooms very quickly. There is no end point as it is a cyclical model.

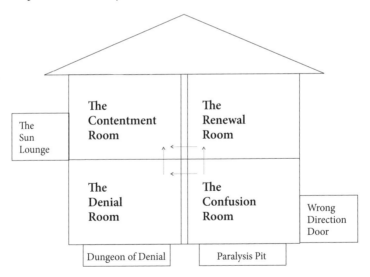

The Contentment Room can be imagined with a sun lounge. The Denial Room has a dungeon (or cellar) for those who are totally stuck in denial. The Confusion Room is the most uncomfortable room and has a pit of paralysis as well as a wrong direction door. In each of the rooms you might find the following behaviours or things being said:

Room	What we say	How we act
Contentment	We're the market leaders	Ignore the outside world
	If it isn't broken, don't fix it	Bureaucratic
	Not invented here	Arrogant
	Management has decided	Uninformed about competitors
	We know our customers	Don't listen to staff
	We have a great track record	Head Office focus
	We're the most profitable	Publish the company history
	Let's decide later	No sense of urgency
	We achieve our budgets	Focus on day-to-day details
	We're the best	Automatic salary increases
Denial	What problem?	Defend the past
	Not my problem	Defend the Present
	HQ doesn't understand	Aggression
	It's an industry trend	Protect the status Quo
	My staff are no good	Maintain taboos
	Competitors are worse	Punish the person bringing bad news
	We've always done it this way	Miss the message
	Our business is different	Don't listen to staff
	If adjusted for ... it's OK	Massage the figures
	It's our customers' fault	Blame everyone else
	It's a short-term issue	Tell stories about past glories

Confusion	How did we get into this mess?	Frustration
	Let's hire some consultant	Depression
	What's happening?	Anger
	What have I done wrong?	Withdrawal
	I've been saying that for years	Blaming management
	We did that years ago	Loss of self-esteem
	It's all my fault	Insecurity
	Help!	No sense of direction
		Irrational behaviour
		Set up committees, task forces
		Never finish things
Renewal	Let's make it happen	Accept responsibility
	Let's do it together	Renewed energy
	Let's tell everybody about it	Enthusiasm
	Now I understand it	Communicate
	It's been tough, but we did it	Listen
	We're stronger now	Learn
	I don't really miss it now	Trust
	It's better than I expected	Delegate
	We have to trust each other	Independent
	We could be better	Accept risk
	Let's beat the challenge	Flexible
		Creative
		Continuously improve
		Set new targets

Source: Prof. Klaus Eckrich (2019) (adapted)

EXERCISE

Reflect upon where your team or organisation is today in terms of their behaviour towards change. Think about the room that would be most useful for you to focus on right now. Think about how you would help people move into the next room or prevent 'stuckness' in Contentment. Write down your ideas.

By following the hyperlink in the reference for Eckrich (2009) at the end of this book the reader can review common strategies he suggests for moving people into the next room.

◆ Organisational Renewal – another perspective

Collins (2001a) wrote a classic leadership book about organisations he had studied which had moved from 'good to great' performance. However less than a decade later a large number of those companies had failed and Collins returned to his original study to figure out what he missed in the original data. He wanted to draw out the predictors of how highly successful organisations can become shipwrecks. In Change House terminology he wanted to understand how an organisation can slip from the Renewal Room into Contentment or worse.

In 'How the Mighty Fall' Collins (2009) shared his wisdom on these good to great has-beens. He found five stages of decline:

STAGE 1 : hubris born of success
STAGE 2 : undisciplined pursuit of more
STAGE 3 : denial of risk and peril
STAGE 4 : grasping for salvation
STAGE 5 : capitulation to irrelevance or death

In the first stage the organisation believed its own story so much that it became complacent. Hubris is arrogance, pride or presumption. There is an Arab proverb which says 'Arrogance diminishes wisdom'. This stage also brings to mind the bible verse:

'Pride goes before destruction, a haughty spirit before a fall'

(Proverbs 16:18, NIV)

In stage two the organisation's leaders pursue a headlong path to acquire, merge and grow. Becoming bigger is their key goal. And the normal processes of due diligence are not enough to protect it from unwise expansion. The organisation becomes unwieldy and fragmented. In stage three the organisation is in the Denial Room unable to acknowledge the enormous risks it is facing. In stage four there is panic to try to find ways to survive as the corporate framework starts to collapse, debts become unmanageable, customers stop buying, income falls and costs become unsustainable. This is the Confusion Room. The final stage is organisational death or ignominy. The organisation has entered the cellar of Despair.

You might now want to reflect on organisations you know and where they might be in this five stage cycle of decline.

➤ Reframing Change solutions
Grint (2010) developed a new way to look at problems particularly in public services. Problems can be categorised as Tame, Critical or Wicked.

Tame Problems
These are management problems which are essentially a puzzle. Standard operating procedures can be utilised to identify appropriate responses and solutions. Tame problems have appeared before and there is a known solution to them. Informal Networks (2009) describe Tame problems as where 'the causes of the problem are known. Experience is a good guide here, and the problems can be tackled by applying known processes through conventional plans and projects'.

Critical Problems

These are associated with a crisis and in the midst of general uncertainty a decisive leader emerges to provide the answer to the problem. Discussion and dissent is minimised. Informal Networks write 'Because these problems threaten the very survival of the organisation in the short term, decisive action is called for, and people are required to follow the call for action in a highly disciplined way. In the absence of time to do a detailed, objective analysis for cause, solutions may be adopted that are based on causes that are assumed to be valid. But a partially successful response is better than standing by idly as the organisation expires'. With this type of problem a 'leader' takes charge, often using an authoritative or even coercive command and control style.

Wicked Problems

These problems are the most challenging and no-one knows how to solve them. These are long term problems and there is time to explore solutions. 'They involve complex, messy and often intractable challenges that can probably rarely be totally eliminated. There are no known solutions, partly because there are no simple, linear causes - the actual causes are themselves complex, ambiguous and often interconnected - multiple causes and causal chains abound' (Informal Networks, 2009). Wicked problems tend to be beyond your experience and are complex rather than complicated. The solutions are fraught with unintended consequences - as you implement a solution something then happens which you did not foresee but which is a result of the solution you implemented. There are no right or wrong answers to Wicked problems - only better or worse developments. Wicked problems are full of uncertainty and ambiguity. Wicked problems are only solved by effective leadership rather than through management.

'Life can only be understood backwards, but it must be lived forwards.'

(Soren Kierkegaard, 1813-55)

The figure below gives a visual representation of the three problem types.

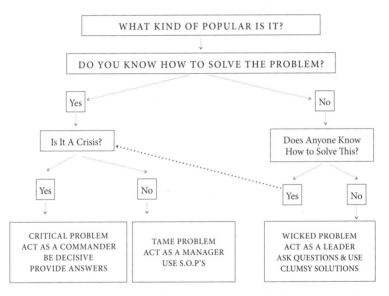

S.O.P. = standard operating procedures

Elegant solutions don't resolve Wicked problems. Leaders need to use collaboration rather than scientific processes to find workable solutions. It is a case of stitching solutions together through a process of experimenting and   learning together. Wicked Problems require Clumsy Solutions.

'Some problems are so complex that you have to be highly intelligent and well informed just to be undecided about them'.

(Peters, 1982)

Clumsy Solutions need appropriate questions, reflection and empathy. They call for using collective intelligence. Grint encourages a shared community of fate (which is different to simply being fatalistic and waiting to see what happens). Leaders developing Clumsy Solutions need to rely on relationships rather than structures to help them. You need to bring in the right people who can help you and these are folk who will demonstrate constructive dissent - they will disagree and debate. In developing Clumsy Solutions leaders need to be aware of the principles of positive deviance:

- Don't assume you have the answer;
- Identify conventional wisdom;
- Identify and analyse 'positive deviants' from that conventional wisdom

Think of a problem you face now as a leader.....
- Is it a Critical, Tame or Wicked problem?
- How do you know?
- What type of approach is needed to find a solution?

You can bring your coaching skills to Wicked problems as they will help you build the questioning, curious and experimenting culture you need to build Clumsy Solutions.

ᕼ Tribal perspectives on the leadership of change
In discussing this book with a colleague I learned of the work of the Nomadic School of Leadership who undertake 'boundary spanning' leadership development between corporate organisations and nomadic tribes in Kenya, Mongolia and Malaysia. In

their work with the Masai in Kenya it is evident that this tribe place great emphasis on community well-being before self-interest. They have a reverence for the wisdom of their elders, who are able to stand back and reflect on decisions needed. The school describe on their website what they call the nomadic mindset:

> '1. Recognise and accept that your environment is changing
> 2. Identify as an agile group that moves towards an opportunity
> 3. Harness the wisdom of your community to make decisions'
> (Nomadic School of Leadership, 2018)

There are clear links here to the effective leadership of change in times of disruption and chaos. This is an example of tribal wisdom in action which can help leaders more generally.

❧ Key wisdom on leadership for change is:

- Change is needed within the leader grappling with organisational change
- Effective leaders need to be able to lead change well
- Change is about winning hearts and minds
- Most change projects fail and this is because they failed to engage the people affected
- Organisations are not machines – they are living systems and a network of human relationships
- When you face chaos you need wise and extraordinary leadership to steer a way through it
- The Change House is a useful tool for change
- Highly successful organisations can become self-satisfied and slowly collapse
- 'Wicked' problems need 'Clumsy' solutions
- When facing change, reframe it as an opportunity and harness the wisdom of your (team) to help you make better decisions

❧ A leadership story to inspire you

'Verily, Allah commands you to establish justice and good-
ness (in the community) and be generous to your relatives,
and he forbids you all evil and indecent deeds and rebellion
against the Truth. This is Allah Who enjoins you so that you
may receive admonition'.

(Qur'an, 16:90)

In the epic Netflix series *'Ertugrul'* the story is told of how this thir-teenth century leader of the tiny Kayi tribe in Anatolia brought the warring Turkmen tribes together against the Mongols - their common enemy. Events were started which led to the formation of the Ottoman Empire, which affected subsequent world history. Ertugrul was a Muslim leader who was passionate about follow-ing the leadership example of the prophet Muhammad. Ertugrul sought justice and fought oppressors. Indeed, he was on the side of the oppressed of whatever faith. Ertugrul is shown planting a plane tree sapling at the start of his migration to contested border lands. In the series he returns again and again to this plane tree which has grown over the years. The tree is a symbol of growth and promise; of patience and persistence. It can also be a metaphor for leader-ship. In the right conditions, substantial growth occurs

Part of my inspiration to write this book came whilst watching *Ertugrul.* It was a phase of history I knew little about and as my wife and I watched the story unfold we became fascinated with a major character, Sheikh Ibn Al-Arabi, who became a spiritual mentor to Ertugrul. Ibn Al-Arabi was a Sufi who followed a rath-er mystical path, which I know is not regarded as 'mainstream' by many Muslims. However, I hope the reader will bear with me for this short leadership story. In the TV production, the wise Sheikh used many metaphors, stories and parables to impart wisdom to Ertugrul, particularly at times of crisis in his leadership. In one of the early episodes of the first season, Ibn al-Arabi gives advice to a downtrodden Ertugrul:

'Life is a school; each one of us is a student and the only teacher we have is God. Manifesting His attributes, He tests us. However, distress and relief, favours and trials all come from Him. Everyone needs to take their own test. You need to be someone who passes the test and knocks down your ego, son. Once this happens, you will be the best (leader).'

Whilst it is a partly fictionalised TV series the lessons are nevertheless very powerful. Patience in the face of trials and setbacks is part of the challenge of leadership. God is working out His purposes as he guides leaders who are in submission to His will. Beekun and Badawi (2009) write 'a deep conviction coupled with patience is essential if a leader wants to challenge the status quo and reform a society or an organization'. Indeed Beekun and Badawi list characteristics of an ethical Islamic leader and each of these was evident in the leadership of Ertugrul:

- 'They act justly, and do not allow their personal feelings to hamper justice
- They take care of those in need, and do so for the love of Allah
- They are steadfast in prayer, and practice charity
- They observe all contracts, and do not break their word
- They are patient and firm, no matter what adversity or personal suffering they may be experiencing'

We can learn much from literature and stories. Leadership wisdom is no exception to this. The story of Ertugrul reinforces the truth that leadership which seeks to transform teams, tribes, organisations or even a nation - such leadership comes with a cost. It calls for vision, courage and patience. Justice will prevail but it may take time. Transformational, caring leadership is the true Islamic model and Ertugrul found that on his own he did not have the resources he needed. He could only achieve the great task he was called to with the help of God. Adair (2010) in *The Leadership of Muhammad* writes: 'Ibn Khaldun takes it as a fundamental principle that human beings are made to cooperate. Central to success in cooperation is what he calls asabiya, the 'group feeling' or 'group spirit'. Having more asabiya makes one group superior to another. Leaders who can command it to best effect will be stronger than their rivals and will even be able to form new dynasties and new states'.

This is precisely what Ertugrul did.

'And we appointed from among them leaders giving guidance under Our command so long as they persevered with patience and continued to have faith in Our signs'

(Qur'an: 32:24)

CHAPTER 12

Conclusion

This book has shared stories of leadership from one of the most challenging environments in the world. These are stories of aspiration against almost overwhelming odds; stories of leaders wanting the best for their family; stories of leadership quietly acted out despite personal danger. These stories of leadership, by ordinary people in extraordinary circumstances, have been undertaken by them with humility and spirituality. *Wisdom for Leadership* has pushed back on the view portrayed in much Western media that Iraq is a country of extremists, bombings, outrages and chaos. It has those things but it is so much more. I have been determined to share a wider narrative.

In 2010 when I stepped off the plane in Erbil for the first time and looked for the face of my contact, he was not there. I decided to wait until we saw his familiar face, ignoring taxi drivers' requests to take us to our hotel. Our host eventually arrived, having been delayed by airport security, and my anxiety reduced. As we drove into the city I saw road signs pointing to Baghdad, Mosul and Kirkuk, some of the most dangerous places on the planet at that time. This was Iraq and I was reminded of the words of the Starbucks barista on our airport layover in Jordan who said, "You are going to Iraq - you are going to die". It was yet another bad view of Iraq, held by someone in a neighbouring country.

However, what I found on that first trip surprised me. I realised my perceptions of the country had been shaped by a view of the worst of it. It was true in part but incomplete. I would learn about leaders who had married across the Sunni -Shia divide and overnight had to flee for their lives after receiving death threats from what they called the 'little people' (i.e. those with small and closed minds). I listened to what it felt like to leave for work each day not knowing if you would return that evening. I was shown chest scars from a close-range assassination attempt. I heard how one Dean negotiated safe release of students taken hostage on his campus, subsequently meeting with a key insurgent leader to agree de-politicising the educational space. At times I had to pinch myself to realise what had just been shared. I came to understand that ordinary folk, in senior leadership positions, were not giving up on their students, their college or their country. Some had experienced their college being destroyed multiple times by shelling or bombings in the Iran- Iraq war, the 1991 Gulf War, the 2003 Gulf War and the 2006-7 insurgency. Each time they had to pick themselves up and start again. The Daesh invasion in 2014 meant it happened again for some.

It was humbling to share these reflections and to see such leadership resilience. These leaders drew their strength from both faith and family. In their worst of times they made sense of the carnage and risk by holding firmly on to God's hand. This was not the faith of 'religion' or partisan affiliation but rather the quiet and determined expression of personal faith and a sense of a higher purpose for their life: 'If today is my last day, then that is God's will for me'. This was not fatalistic giving up but more a sense, amidst the chaos spread by evil men, that God was still there and there was work to do.

I came to understand that the motivation of these men and women leaders was much the same as for leaders in the Western educational organisations I had worked with. They wanted the best outcomes for students and the best opportunities for their families. They wanted to live a life in which relationships were valued and nurtured. They wanted to be the best possible leader in their situation. And they were doing this in spite of limited resources, unreliable power supplies, inadequate health systems, fledgling government processes and political instabilities.

I visited Iraq ten times and additionally worked with my Iraqi delegates in Istanbul and the UK. I left a part of my heart with the people of this incredible country. It is a troubled nation and is indeed, at times, chaotic. It is plagued by corruption. But it is also rich in culture and history, oil resources and, most importantly, human capital. It is the birthplace of civilisation, agriculture and the three great Abrahamic faiths. It is a country where ordinary people share their food, friendship and stories. It is a land where they dream of peace and stability for their children.

I experienced a hunger for collaborative leadership models from men and women, Kurds, Arabs and Turkmen, Sunni, Shia and Christians. Their willingness to learn from one another was humbling. In a workshop in Sulaymaniyah the southern Arab delegates insisted we visited nearby Halabjah, scene of the genocidal chemical attack in 1988 in which 5000 Kurdish men, women and children had been murdered by Sadaam Hussein. The pilgrimage we made together was itself a symbol of reconciliation and hope.

'In order for evil to flourish, all that is required is for good men to do nothing'

(President Kennedy, 1961, citing Edmund Burke)

These good men and women of Iraq did something. They are the hidden face of Iraq, striving to make a difference. We can learn much from them about leadership in adversity. The effects of the DQP and HQP programmes are still being felt today as participants continue to develop and coach others across Iraq (British Council, 2018). The seeds of leadership development which we were privileged to sow are reaping a big harvest. I believe that the programme prospered because it was approached in faith by participants and tutors alike. It was delivered with a shared hope for the future. The evidence of positive impact on individuals and their organisations abounds. I hope, dear reader, that you will be able to use some of the leadership ideas, models and concepts in this book to help you further develop your own wisdom for leadership to create amazing workplaces and high performance teams.

'God will not change the condition of a people until they change it themselves'

(Qur'an 13:11)

Useful (and mainly) Free Online Resources

BOX OF CRAYONS
https://boxofcrayons.com/

- Coaching resources from Michael Bungay Stanier
- Bungay Stanier has lots of free resources available at The-CoachingHabit.com
- Wonderful short animation about Great Work
- Do More Great Work by Michael Bungay Stanier on YouTube: https://www.youtube.com/watch?v=1o3arNIFGU0&ab_channel=WorkmanPublishing

CMI SITE
https://www.managers.org.uk/

- Chartered Management Institute – UK based but with international reach

EMPATHY

- Brene Brown's short animation on empathy
- Brene Brown on Empathy on YouTube. https://www.youtube.com/watch?v=1Evwgu369Jw

IEDP
https://www.iedp.com/about-us/

- Range of free resources on leadership development including *Developing Leaders* journal

LENCIONI
Resources for team health at
https://www.tablegroup.com/topics-and-resources/teamwork-5-dys-functions/

MANAGEMENT INNOVATION EXCHANGE
https://www.managementexchange.com/

- Forum for exploring and exchanging ideas on innovative approaches to embedded leadership and other problems (see Nelson, 2011a)

RSA ANIMATED
https://www.thersa.org/discover/videos/rsa-animate

- The Royal Society of Arts 'Animate' series was conceived as an innovative, accessible and unique way of illustrating and sharing the world-changing ideas from the RSA's free public events programme. Includes:
- Dan Pink on motivation
  https://www.thersa.org/discover/videos/rsa-animate/2010/04/rsa-animate---drive

THE HOT SPOTS MOVEMENT
https://www.hotspotsmovement.com/

- Prof. Lynda Gratton's growing body of knowledge on the changing nature of work, who works out of London Business School

TED
https://www.ted.com/

- Short video talks by leading thinkers on a wide range of topics including those relevant to leadership and change
- You might want to start with this one from Simon Sinek
  https://www.ted.com/talks/simon_sinek_how_great_leaders_inspire_action

CONTACT TONY
You can follow Tony Nelson on twitter @TonyNelson7

Glossary

AoC   Association of Colleges in UK

CMI   Chartered Management Institute

CMgr   Chartered Manager

DQP   Deans Qualifying Programme (Technical Colleges – many are now Technical Universities)

FCMI   Fellow of the Chartered Management Institute

FTE   Iraqi Foundation for Technical Education – there were three organisations each responsible for technical education in their respective geographies of Baghdad (covering most of Iraq) and two in Iraqi Kurdistan region in Erbil and   Sulaymaniyah

MCMI   Member of the Chartered Management Institute

HQP   Heads Qualifying Programme (Vocational Schools)

LTF   Leadership Trust Foundation in UK

PQP   Principals Qualifying Programme – for the leaders of UKs Further Education Colleges, Sixth Form and Specialist Colleges

Rawabit   *(Arabic meaning partnership or collaboration)* Once the 2003 war ended, vocational education was presented with the opportunity of re-connecting with the outside world after 30 years of isolation from new ideas and embargos of economic development. But as the country descended into post-war chaos, colleges were stripped by looters. Colleges faced the challenge of equipping young people and adults with the vocational skills desperately needed to rebuild local economies. Society was divided and infrastructure decimated. Few leaders ever face such challenges in their lifetime and Rawabit has been a lifeline to Iraq's Foundation for Technical Education. Rawabit was set up in 2004 by the Iraqi FTE, a group of UK FE colleges, the Association of Colleges and other UK agencies. It subsequently attracted funds from the UK government (now Department for Business, Innovation and Skills) and UNESCO. More than 600 senior managers and staff from across Iraq (including many women) have benefited from practical programmes to raise skills, develop strategy and make the curriculum more responsive to market needs. Many of these have visited the UK on study visits to twinned Colleges in England and N. Ireland or attended conferences in Istanbul or Jordan to share two-way learning and exchange ideas. The experience of N. Ireland resonated deeply with Iraqi colleagues who are working to overcome sectarian, political, tribal and religious divisions on their campuses. Iraqi colleges have supported former insurgents and prisoners to leave violence behind and learn trades to channel their energies productively.

References

Ackermann F., Eden C., (2005) *The Practice of Making Strategy*, London, Sage

Adair, J. (1973), *Action Centred Leadership*, London, McGraw-Hill Education.

Adair. J. (1989) *Great Leaders* Guildford The Talbot Adair Press

Adair, J (2010) *The Leadership of Muhammad* London Kogan Page

Adair J., (2003 b) *The Inspirational Leader* London Kogan Page

Adair (2016) Video lecture [YouTube] 6 October, 2016. Available at: https://www.youtube.com/watch?v=EoADvUS93Cg [Accessed 2 Nov, 2019].

Adair, J. (2018) *Lessons in Leadership: 12 key concepts* London, Bloomsbury

Adair, J. (2020) *The Art of Judgment : 10 steps to becoming a more effective decision-maker*, London, Bloomsbury

Al-Azami, N. (2019) *Muhammad : 11 Leadership Qualities That Changed The Worlds* Swansea, Claritas Books

Al Buraey, M. (1985) *Administrative Development: An Islamic Perspective*, London, KPI

Al-husseini, S. J.(2014) *The Impact of Leadership Style on Innovation in Iraq's Higher Education Institutions: The Role of Knowledge Sharing.* Thesis (PhD) Plymouth University

Al Islam (2019) 'The Battle of the Trench' Available at : https://www.al-islam.org/restatement-history-islam-and-muslims-sayyid-ali-ashgar-razwy/battle-trench [Accessed: 9 Dec, 2019].

Al- Muhajir, B., (2017) *Sa'ad ibn Mu'adh ... A Hero Amongst Heroes of the Muslims and a Role Model for the Muslim Army Officers of Today* Available at: http://www.khilafah.com/saad-ibn-muadh-a-hero-amongst-heroes-of-the-muslims-and-a-role-model-for-the-muslim-army-officers-of-today/ [Accessed: 9 Dec, 2019]

Alimo-Metcalfe, B. (1995), "An investigation of female and male constructs of leadership and empowerment", *Women in Management Review*, 10. 2, pp.3-8.

Andersen, J.A. (2000), "Leadership and leadership research", in Dahiya, D.F. (Eds), *Current Issues in Business Disciplines, Vol. 5: Management II*, New Delhi, Spellbound Publications.

Ankerberg, J., & Burroughs, D. (2008). *What's the Big Deal About Other Religions?:*

Answering the Questions about Their Beliefs and Practices. Harvest House Publishers.

Antanocopoulou, E., Bento, R. (1994) 'Learning Leadership in practice' in J. Storey (ed) (2004). *Leadership in Organizations: Current Issues and Trends*, London, Routledge, pp81-102

Augsburger, D. (1982) *Caring Enough to Hear and Be Heard: How to Hear and How to Be Heard in Equal Communication* Ada, Michigan, Baker Group Publishing

Avery, G. (2004) *Understanding Leadership*, London, Sage Publications.

Badawy, M.K (1980), "Styles of mid-eastern managers", *California Management Review*, 22, 2, 51-8.

Bass, B. (1990a). From transactional to transformational leadership: learning to share the vision. *Organizational Dynamics*, 8, 3, Winter, 19-31.

Bass, B. (1990b) Bass and Stodgill's Handbook of Leadership, New York, N.Y., Simon and Schuster Inc.

Bass, B. Avolio, B. (1990) *Developing Transformational Leadership: Multifactor Leadership Questionnaire,* San Francisco, CA., Consulting Psychologists Press.

Bass, B.M., Avolio, B.J. (1995), *Multifactor Leadership Questionnaire for Research,* Palo Alto, CA., Mind Garden.

Beech, N., Cairns, G., Livingstone, H., Lockyer, C., Tsoukas, H. (2001) *Managing People In Organisations* Vol 1 & 2 USGSB Strathclyde University of Strathclyde Graduate Business School

Beech N., Crane O., (1999) *High Performance Teams and a Climate of Community* Working Paper 99/4 Strathclyde University of Strathclyde Graduate Business School

Beekun,R.I, Badawi,J. (1999) *Leadership – an Islamic perspective* Maryland Amana Publications

Beekun.,I., Badawi,J. (2009) *Leadership: An Islamic Perspective,* Beltsville, Maryland, amana publications

Bennis, W., (1959) *The Problem of Authority,* Johnson Graduate School of Management, Cornell University

Bennis W., (1997) 'The Secrets of Great Groups' *Leader to Leader.* 3 (Winter) 29-33

Bennis, W., Nanus, B. (1985), *Leaders: The Strategies for Taking Charge,* New York, NY, Harper & Row

Bevan S., Cowling M., Horner L., Isles N., Turner N., (2005) 'Cracking the Performance Code : How Firms Succeed' Available at: www.theworkfoundation.com

Blake, R.R., Mouton, J.S. (1964), *Managerial Grid,* Houston, TX, Gulf.

Bion, W. R., (1991) *A Memoir of the Future,* London, Karnac Books

Birkinshaw, J. (2010) *Reinventing Management* London Jossey Bass

Bolman L.G., Deal T.E., (1991) 'Leadership and Management Effectiveness: A Multi- frame, Multi-sector Analysis' *Human Resource*

Management ,30, 509-534

Bolman L.G., Deal T.E., (1992a) 'Leading and Managing : Effects of Context, Culture and Gender' *Education Administration Quarterly* *28,314-329*

Bolman L.G., Deal T.E., (1992b) ''Reframing leadership: The Effects of Leaders' Images of Leadership' In K.E. Clark, and D. Campbell (eds), *Impact of Leadership* Greensboro, N.C.: Center for Creative Leadership

Bolman L.G., Deal T.E., (1997) *Reframing Organisations* 2nd edition San Francisco Jossey-Bass

British Council (2018) *TVET leadership and teacher development in Iraq.* Available at: https://www.britishcouncil.org/education/skills-employability/success-stories/TVET-leadership-and-teacher-development-Iraq [Accessed: 21 Nov, 2019].

Brown, P., Dzendrowskyj, T. (2018) 'Sorting out an emotional muddle: Insights from neuroscience on the organizational value of emotions', *Developing Leaders Issue 29:Spring 2018,* Available at: https://www.developingleadersquarterly.com/fb/Developing-Leaders-issue-29-Spring-2018/26/#zoom=z [Accessed 13 Dec, 2019}.

Bruch, H, Vogel, B. (2011) *Fully Charged: How Great Leaders Boost Their Organization's Energy and Ignite High Performance* Brighton, Massachusetts Harvard Business Review Press

Bungay Stanier, M., (2010), *Do More Great Work*, New York, Workman Books

Bungay Stanier, M., (2016) *The Coaching Habit: Say Less, Ask more, and Change the way you Lead Forever*, Toronto, Box of Crayons Press

Burns J. M., (1978) *Leadership,* N.Y., Harper Row

Cambridge Dictionary (2019) Available at: https://dictionary.cambridge.org/dictionary/english/wisdom[Accessed: 11 Dec, 2019].

Carlin, J. (2008), *Playing The Enemy*, London, Atlantic Books

Child, J. (1976) 'Participation, organization, and social cohesion' *Human Relations* 29 (5), 429-451

Chynoweth, C. (2011) 'Be a leader, not a dictator'. *The Sunday Times* 03 July 2011 Appointments p5 Available at https://www.thetimes.co.uk/article/be-a-leader-not-a-dictator-22f5r5z00ds [Accessed: 06 November, 2019].

Cleary, M. (1995), *'You're the coach'*, Credit Union Management

Collingwood, H. (2001), 'Personal histories', *Harvard Business Review*, pp.27-38.

Collins, J. (2001), *Good To Great*, London, Random House Business Books.

Collins, J. (2001), "Level 5 leadership. The triumph of humility and fierce resolve", *Harvard Business Review*, pp.67-76.

Collins J.C, and Porras J.I., (1994) *Built to last: Successful Habits of Visionary Companies* New York Harper Collins

Collins, J. (2009) *How the Mighty Fall* rh business books

Conger, J (1990), "The dark side of leadership", in Hickman, G.R (Eds),*Leading Organizations, Perspectives for a New Era*, London, Sage.

Cooper R., Sawaf A., (1997) *Emotional Intelligence in Business* London Orion Books Ltd

Covey, S (1992) *The 7 Habits of Highly Effective People.* London. Simon & Schuster UK Ltd

Covey, F (2020) *Habit 2: Begin with the End in Mind*, Available at: https://www.franklincovey.com/the-7-habits/habit-2.html [Accessed: 7 January, 2020].

Covey, S. (2008) *The Speed of Trust: The One Thing That Changes Everything.* New York. Free Press

Csikszentmihalyi, M. (2002), *Flow: The Psychology of Happiness: The Classic Work on How to Achieve Happiness,* London, Random House Group

Cuncic, A. (2020) *How to Practice Active Listening* Available at: https://

www.verywellmind.com/what-is-active-listening-3024343, [Accessed 07 January, 2020].

Dia, M (1994), "Indigenous management practices: lessons for Africa's management in the '90s", in Serageldine, I, Taboroff, J (Eds),*Culture and Development in Africa*, Washington, DC, World Bank.

De Rond, M., 2009 *The Last Amateurs* London Icon

Diehl, M., (2008) *Mindset Works* (assess your mindset) Available at: http://blog.mindsetworks.com/what-s-my-mindset?view=quiz [Accessed: 19 Nov, 2019].

Druskat V.U., Wolff S.B., (2001) *Building the Emotional Intelligence of Groups*

republished in Harvard Business Review On Teams that Succeed (2004) Boston, Harvard Business School

Druskat V.U., Wheeler J.V., (2004) How to lead a Self Managing Team *MIT Sloan Management Review Summer 2004 v45 i4 p65 (3)*

Dulewicz, V. (1999), "Emotional intelligence and corporate leadership", Inaugural Lecture, Henley-on-Thames, Oxford, Henley Management College.

Dulewicz, C., Young, M., Dulewicz, V. (2005), "The relevance of emotional intelligence for leadership performance", *Journal of General Management*, 30. 3, pp.71-86.

Dweck,C. ,(2006) *Mindset: The New Psychology of Success,* NY, Ballantine Books

Eaton, J., Johnson, R., (2001) *Coaching Successfully*: Essential Managers series , London, Dorling-Kindersley

Eckrich, E. (2019) *Change Leadership* Available at: http://www.changehouse.de/dokumente/Fol_ChangeLeadership_engl.pdf [Accessed: 7 Nov, 2019]

Edmondson A., Bohmer R., Pisano G., (2001)*Speeding Up Team Learning,* republished in Harvard Business Review On Teams that Succeed

(2004) Boston, Harvard Business School

Edwards G., Winter P.K., Bailey J., (2002) *Leadership in Management* Ross on Wye The Leadership Trust

Eraut, M. (1994) *Developing Professional Knowledge And Competence* Abingdon on Thames, Routledge

Eraut, M. (2004b) Practice based evidence, in: G. Thomas & R. Pring (Eds) Evidence-based practice

in education (Maidenhead, Open University Press), 91±101.

Eraut, M. (2004b) Practice based evidence, in: G. Thomas & R. Pring (Eds) Evidence-based practice

in education (Maidenhead, Open University Press), 91±101.

Eraut, M. (2004b) Practice based evidence, in: G. Thomas & R. Pring (Eds) Evidence-based practice

in education (Maidenhead, Open University Press), 91±101.

Faris, N., Abdalla, M. (2018) *Leadership in Islam*: Thoughts, Processes and Solutions in Australian Organizations London Palgrave Macmillan

Fiedler, F.E. (1967), *A Theory of Leadership Effectiveness*, New York, NY, McGraw-Hill.

Feiner M.C., (2002) Financial Times, *Mastering Leadership* series Nov 15 p 5

Fineman, S. (1997), "Emotion and management learning", *Management Learning*, 28, 1, pp.13-25.

Frankl, V. (2004) *Man's Search for Meaning* Reading, UK, Random House

Friedman, H. H. and Friedman, L. W. (2019) 'What Went Wrong? Lessons in Leadership from Solomon, the Bible's Wisest and Worst Ruler,' *The Journal of Values-Based Leadership*: Vol. 12 : Iss. 1 , Article 5. Available at: http://dx.doi.org/10.22543/0733.121.1237 [Accessed: 14 Dec, 2019].

Fuller A., Ashton D., Felstead A., Unwin L., Walters S., Quinn M., (2003) *The Impact of Informal Learning at Work on Business Productivity* London DTi

Gallwey, T., 1986 *The Inner Game of Tennis* London Pan

Gardner, H. (1993), *Frames of Mind*, New York, NY, Basic Books.

Garvin, D.A. & Roberto, M.A. (2001). What you don't know about making decisions. *Harvard Business Review*, 79(8), 108-116.

Gilbert-Smith, D. (2003) *Winning Hearts and Minds*, London, Penn Press Publishers Ltd

Gill R., (2001) *Essays on Leadership* Ross on Wye Leadership Trust

Gill, R. (2006), *Theory and Practice of Leadership*, London, Sage Publications.

Goffee, R., Jones, G. (2000), "Why should anyone be led by you?", *Harvard Business Review*, pp.63-70

Goldsmith, M. (2008) *What got you here won't get you there* Profile Books London

Goleman, D. (1995), *Emotional Intelligence: Why It Can Matter More than IQ*, London, Bloomsbury Publishing,.

Goleman, D. (1998), *Working with Emotional Intelligence*, London., Bloomsbury Publishing,.

Goleman, D.(2000) 'Leadership That Gets Results' *Harvard Business Review* March-April 2000

Goleman, D. (2001), "An EI-based theory of performance", in Cherniss, C., Goleman, D. (Eds),*The Emotionally Intelligent Workplace*, San Francisco, CA., Jossey-Bass.

Goleman, D., Boyatzis, R., McKee, A. (2002), *Primal Leadership*, Boston, MA, Harvard Business School Press,.

Goleman, D. (2002a) *The New Leaders*. Little, Brown

Goleman D., (2002b) 'Leading Resonant Teams' *Leader to Leader* 25 (Summer) 24-30

Goleman D., Boyatzis R., Mckee A., (2003) *The New Leaders : Transforming the Art of Leadership into the Science of Results* London Time Warner

Gratton. L. (2007) *Hot Spots* London Prentice Hall

Gratton. L., (2012) *Glow* London, ReadHowYouWant

Greenleaf, R., (1970) *The Servant as Leader*, Sutton, The Greenleaf Centre for Servant Leadership

Greenleaf, R. (1977) *Servant Leadership* New York: Paulist Press

Grint K. (2010) 'Wicked Problems and Clumsy Solutions: The Role of Leadership', In: Brookes S., Grint K. (eds) *The New Public Leadership Challenge*. London, Palgrave Macmillan

Gumbel, N. (2019) *BIOY* app Available at: https://apps.apple.com/gb/app/bible-in-one-year/id504133402 [Accessed: 29 October, 2020].

Hammarskjold,D. (1964) *Markings,* New York, Ballantine

Handy C., (1976), *Understanding Organisations*, 4th edition, London Penguin

Harding R., Cowling M., Turner N., (2003) *The Missing Link: From Productivity to Performance* London The Work Foundation

Hartley, J. (2002)'Organisational change and development' in Peter Warr (ed) , *Psychology at Work,* London, Penguin Books

Hersey, P., Blanchard, K.H. (1969), "Life cycle theory of leadership", *Training and Development Journal*, 23. 5, pp.26-34.

Hersey, P., Blanchard, K.H. (1993), *Management of Organizational Behavior; Utilising Human Resources*, Englewood Cliffs, NJ., Prentice-Hall.

Hertzberg, F. (1959) *The Motivation to Work* New York: John Wiley & Sons

Hesselbein F., Goldsmith M., Beckhard R., (eds), (1996), *The Leader of the Future*, New York The Drucker Foundation

Higgs, M.J., Dulewicz, S.V. (2000), "Emotional intelligence, leadership and culture", paper presented at Emotional Intelligence Conference, London., .

Higgs, M.J., Rowland, D. (2001), "Developing change leadership capability. The impact of a development intervention", *Henley Working Paper Series*, HWP 2001/004.,

Higgs, M.J., Dulewicz, S.V. (2002), *Making Sense of Emotional Intelligence*, 2nd ed., Windsor, NFER-Nelson.

Higgs, M.J. (2003), "How can we make sense of leadership in the 21st century?", *Leadership & Organization Development Journal*, 24, 5, pp. 273-284.

Hofstede, G (1980), *Cultures' Consequences*, Beverley Hills, CA, Sage

Hofstede, G (1984), "Cultural dimensions in management and planning", *Asia Pacific Journal of Management*, 1, 81-99.

Hofstede, G. (1991), *Cultures and Organizations : Software of the Mind*, New York, Mcgraw-Hill

Hofstede, G. (1999) 'Problems remain but theories will change: the universal and the specific in 21st century global management', *Organizational Dynamics*, 28 (1), 34-43

Hofstede, G., Hofstede G.J., (2005), *Cultures and Organizations : Software of the Mind* 2nd edn.,New York, McGraw-Hill

Hogan, R., Hogan, J. (2001), "Assessing leadership: a view from the dark side", *International Journal of Selection and Development*, 9, 1/2, pp.40-51.

Horne M., Stedman Jones D., (2001) ' *Leadership – the challenge for all?*' London Institute of Management

House, R.J., Podaskoff, P.M. (1994), "Leadership effectiveness: past perspectives and future direction for research", in Greenberg, J. (Eds),*Organizational Behavior: The State of the Science*, Hillsdale, NJ, Lawrence Erlbaum Associates, pp.45-82.

Huxham C., Vangen S., (2004) Doing things Collaboratively: realizing the advantage or succumbing to inertia?' *Organisational Dynamics, Vol 33/2, 190-201-* taken from USGSB Managing reader 2002 Strathclyde University of Strathclyde Graduate Business School

Huxham C., Beech N., (2003) 'Contrary prescriptions: Recognizing good practice tensions in management' , *Organization Studies*, Vol 24, 69-92 - taken from USGSB Managing reader 2002 Strathclyde University of Strathclyde Graduate Business School

Janis, I.L., (1982) *Groupthink* Boston Houghton Mifflin

Infinite light, (2019) *Consultation* Available at: http://www.infinitelight. org/aspects-of-his-life/731-consultation.html [Accessed: 9 Dec, 2019].

Informal Networks, (2009) *Wicked problems and the role of leadership,* Available at : https://informalnetworks.co.uk/wp-content/uploads/2014/09/Wicked_problems_and_the_role_of_leadership.pdf [Accessed: 20 Nov, 2019].

Institute for Leadership and Management (2014) *'The truth about trust: Honesty and integrity at work'.* Available at : file:///C:/Users/User1/ Downloads/TruthAboutTrust.pdf [Accessed: 3 Dec, 2019].

Islam Awareness (2019) *'Ibn Kathir: Story of Prophet Dawud/David'* Available at: https://www.islamawareness.net/Prophets/dawud.html [Accessed : 22 Nov, 2019).

Islamic Centre of Redmond, (2019) *'Story of Ikrimah Ibn Abi Jahl'* Available at : https://www.redmondmosque.org/story-of-ikrimah-ibn-abi-jahl/ [Accessed: 9 Dec, 2019].

Jackson, P.Z., McKergow,M., (2002), *The Solutions Focus,* London, Nicholas Brealey Publishing

Janis, I.L. (1982a), *Groupthink*, second edition, Yale MA Houghton Miflin,

Janis, I.L., (1982b), "Introduction: why so many miscalculations?" in *Groupthink: psychological studies of policy decisions and fiascoes*, 2nd edition, Yale, Houghton Miflin, pp.2-13

Jaffee, D. (2001), *Organization Theory – Tension and Change*, New York,

NY, McGraw-Hill.

Janssen, C. F. (1996) *The Four Rooms of Change,* Sweden, Liber

JISC (2019) *Complexity Theory* Available at: https://www.jisc.ac.uk/guides/change-management/complexity-theory [Accessed 10 Dec, 2019]

Jobs, S. (2011) *Steve Jobs: His Own Words and Wisdom,* Cupertino CA, Cupertino Silicon Valley Press

Johnson G., (1988) 'Rethinking Incrementalism', *Strategic Management Journal,* Vol 9, 75-91 - taken from USGSB Managing reader 2002 Strathclyde University of Strathclyde Graduate Business School

Jordan, P.J., Troth, A.C. (2004), "Managing emotions during team problem solving: emotional intelligence and conflict resolution", *Human Performance,* 17. 2, pp.195-218.

Jones P., Palmer J., Osterwell C., Whitehead D., (1996) *Delivering Exceptional Performance : Aligning the Potential of Organisations, Teams and Individuals* London Pitman

Kaplan R.S., Norton D.P. (1992) *The Balanced Scorecard – Measures That Drive Performance* republished in Harvard Business Review on Measuring Corporate Performance Boston, Harvard Business School Press

Kathir, I. Ibn (2019) *Stories of the Prophets (pbuh),* Italy, Amazon Italia Logistica

Katzenbach, J.R., Smith D.K., 1993 "The team performance curve" Chapter 5 in *The wisdom of teams: creating the high-performance organisation,* Boston, Harvard Business School Press, pp. 87-108

Katzenbach J.R., Smith D.K (1993) *The Wisdom of Teams – Creating the High-Performance Organisation,* Boston Harvard Business School Press

Katzenbach J.R., (1998) '*Making teams Work at the Top*' Leader to Leader. 7 (Winter) 32-38

Katzenbach J.R ., Smith D.K., (2004) *The Discipline of Teams* republished in Harvard Business Review On Teams that Succeed, Boston, Harvard

Business School Press

Kennedy, R. (1961) *Documents on Disarmament 1961*, [May 17, 1961: Address by President Kennedy to the Canadian Parliament {Extracts}], United States Arms Control and Disarmament Agency, Publication 5, Released August 1962, Washington, D.C. (HathiTrust full view)

Kernan M.A., (2003) *Team Learning- Unlocking organisational Potential* London The Talent Foundation

Key Differences (2019) *Difference Between Knowledge and Wisdom.* Available at:

https://keydifferences.com/difference-between-knowledge-and-wisdom.html [Accessed: 25 Nov, 2019].

King, P. & Eaton, J. (1999) *Coaching for Results* Available at: https://cemi. com.au/sites/all/publications/King%20and%20Eaton%201999%20 Coaching.pdf [Accessed: 10 Dec, 2019].

Kirkpatrick D.L., (1996) *Evaluating Training Programs: The Four Levels*, Berret-Koehler, San Francisco

Kotter, J. P. (1990), *A Force for Change: How Leadership Differs From Management,* New York, NY., Free Press.

Kouzes and Posner (1998), *Encouraging the Heart*, San Francisco, CA. Jossey-Bass.

Kubler-Ross, E. (1969) *On Death & Dying: What the Dying Have to Teach Doctors, Nurses, Clergy & Their Own Families,* NY, Scribner

Lawlor E.E., (2004) Leading a Virtuous-Spiral Organisation Spring 2004,32 p32 -40 *Leader to Leader*

Leadership Trust, (2003), *Pocket Book Tutor,* Ross on Wye, Leadership Trust (Training) Ltd

Lencioni, P, (2005), *Overcoming the 5 Dysfunctions of a Team; A Field Guide*, San Francisco, Jossey-Bass

Lopes, P.N., Salovey, P., Cote, S., Beers, M. (2005), "Emotion regulation ability and the quality of social interaction", *Emotion*, 5.1, pp.113-8.

Lucas, W., (2010) *New Kinds Of Smart: How The Science Of Learnable Intelligence Is Changing Education: How the Science of Learnable Intelligence is Changing Education* Milton Keynes Open University Press

McCall, M.W., Sergist, C.A. (1980), *In Pursuit of the Manager's Job: Building on Mintzberg*, Greensboro, NC., Centre for Creative Learning.

McGregor, D. (1960) *The Human Side of Enterprise* New York, McGraw-Hill Education

Machiavelli, N. (2017) *The Prince* , Scotts Valley, CA. , CreateSpace Independent Publishing Platform

Management Innovation Exchange (2019) Available at: https://www.managementexchange.com/ [Accessed 9 Dec, 2019].

Mandela, N. (1995) *'The Long Walk to Freedom'* London, Abacus

Mandell, B., Pherwani, S. (2003), "Relationship between emotional intelligence and transformational leadership style: a gender comparison", *Journal of Business and Psychology*, 17. 3, pp.387-404.

March J.G., (1994) *A Primer on Decision Making: How decisions Happen* Chapter 1, 1-35 - taken from USGSB Managing reader 2002 Strathclyde University of Strathclyde Graduate Business School

Maslow, A. (1962), *Towards a Psychology of Being*, New York, Van Nostrand.

Mather C., (2004) *Leadership and learning – in decline and in denial?* A lecture I attended on 18 May www.shell.com/speeches

Mather C., (2004) *Leadership and learning – in decline and in denial?* A lecture on 18 May Available at: www.shell.com/speeches

Mayer, J.D., Salovey, P. (1997), "What is emotional intelligence?", in Salovey, P., Sluyter, D.J. (Eds),*Emotional Development and Emotional Intelligence*, New York, NY., Basic Books.

Mayo Clinic (2019) *'Stress relief from laughter? It's no joke'.* Available at : https://www.mayoclinic.org/healthy-lifestyle/stress-management/in-depth/stress-relief/art-20044456 [Accessed: 3 Dec, 2019].

Metcalfe, B.D. & Mimouni, F. (eds) (2011) *Leadership Development in the Middle East* Cheltenham, EE

Meyer C., (1994) 'How the Right measures help teams Excel' republished in Harvard Business Review On Teams that Succeed (2004) Boston, Harvard Business School

Mintzberg H., (1975) 'The Manager's job; folklore and fact' *Harvard Business Review* July-August

Mohammad, J., Mohammad Ibrahim, A. L., Abdul Salam, Z., Jamil, R., & Quoquab, F.

(2015). Towards developing a conceptual framework of Islamic leadership: The role of Taqwa as a moderator. *International Journal of Innovation and Business*

Strategy, *3*(1).

Moon, J. (2006) *Learning Journals,* Abingdon on Thames, Routledge

Morris S., Willcocks G., Knasel E., (1995) *How to Lead a Winning Team* The Institute of Management London Pitman

Muna, F.A (1980), *The Arab Executive*, London, Macmillan.

Nelson, A., & Peel, D., (2005a) *Evaluation of the LSC London Central's High Performance Programme,* unpublished, London

Nelson, T. (2005b) *Getting Out of The Way* Dissertation (MBA), unpublished, Strathclyde University

Nelson, T. (2010) *Getting out of the Way* Available at: https://www.managementexchange.com/story/getting-out-way [Accessed: 6 Nov, 2019].

Nelson, T. (2011a) *Arabian Knights: A tale of leadership transformation with Iraqi Deans* Available at: https://www.managementexchange.com/story/serving-lead-transforming-leadership-iraqi-college-deans [Accessed: 6 Nov, 2019].

Nelson, T. & Peel,D. (2011b) 'Leadership Skills for the New Iraq: A program for College Deans'. *Developing Leaders*. Issue 5. 2011 pp 49-54 Available at: https://developingleadersquarterly.com/fb/Developing-Leaders-issue-5-2011/48/ , [Accessed: 11 Dec, 2019].

Nelson, T. (2011c) *Deans Qualifying Programme: An Evaluation* Available at: https://www.managementexchange.com/sites/default/files/media/posts/documents/DQP_An_Evaluation.pdf [Accessed : 6 Nov, 2019].

Nelson, A. (editor) (2012) *A guide to thinking about leadership: leading and developing people.* Rawabit, Unpublished.

Nomadic School of Leadership (2018) *'What is a nomadic mindset?'* Available at: http://www.nomadicschoolofbusiness.com/solutions/why-nomads-new/ , [Accessed: 13 Dec, 2019]

Oppland, M., (2019) *8 ways to create Flow according to Mihaly Csikszentmihalyo*

Available at : https://positivepsychology.com/mihaly-csikszentmihalyi-father-of-flow/ [Accessed: 18 Nov, 2019].

Peterson, R.S. (2017a) 'Global leaders can learn from Arab leadership styles' *Saudi Gazette* (Online) Available at: http://saudigazette.com.sa/article/513858 [Accessed: 23 Nov, 2019].

Peterson, R.S. (2017b) 'Leading teams: tactics inspired by the Middle East' *London Business School* Available at: https://www.london.edu/lbsr/leading-teams-tactics-inspired-by-the-middle-east [Accessed: 23 Nov, 2019]

Perry B., (1984) *Enfield: A High Performance System* Digital Equipment Corporation Educational Services Development and Publishing

Peter, L.J. (1982) *Peter's Almanac,* N.Y., William Morrow & Co

Pink, D. (2010) *Drive* Edinburgh Canongate Books

Pfeffer J.,(1998) 'The Real Keys to High Performance' *Leader to Leader.* 8 (Spring) 23-29

Plato (1997) *The Republic,* Ware, Wordsworth Classics of World Literature

Pugh D.S., Hickson D.J., (1989) 'The Management of Organisations', *Writers on Organisations,* 4th edn 84, 91-101 and 5th edn 95-129 – taken from USGSB Managing reader 2002

Polley D., Ribbens B., (1998) 'Sustaining Self-Managed teams: a process to team wellness', *Team Performance Management, Vol 4, No1*

Qu'ran (2000) Translated by Abdullah Yusuf Ali, Ware, Wordsworth Editions Ltd

Qouteinvestigator.com (2020) 'Serenity Prayer' Available at: https://quoteinvestigator.com/2019/12/24/serenity/ [Accessed: 06 January, 2020].

Rajan A., (2004a) Master Class lecture on *High Performance Culture* 6 April London

Rajan A., (2004b) HTI Issues Paper 5 *All That Jazz – Managing change to create high performance cultures* Warwick HTI

Rajan A., (1996) *Leading People* Tunbridge Wells CREATE

Reading, S.G (1990), *The Spirit of Chinese Capitalism,* Berlin and New York, NY, Walter de Gruyter.

Rogers, C. (1959). A theory of therapy, personality and interpersonal relationships as developed in the client-centered framework. In (ed.) S. Koch, *Psychology: A study of a science. Vol. 3: Formulations of the person and the social context.* New York: McGraw Hill.

Salaman G., (1995) *Managing* Chapters 3, 5, &7, Buckingham, Open University Press

Salovey, P., Mayer, J.D. (1990), "Emotional intelligence", *Imagination, Cognition and Personality,* 9. pp.185-211.

Santayana, G. (1905) *The Life of Reason: Reason in Common Sense vol. 1,* N.Y., Dover Publications Inc.; New ed of 1905 ed edition (1 Feb. 1980)

Seddon J., (1992) *I want you to Cheat!* Buckingham Vanguard Press

Seldon, A. (2009) *Trust – how we lost it and how to get it back,* London, Biteback Publishing Ltd

Sessions, R. (1950) 'How a 'Difficult' Composer Gets That Way' *New York Times* 8 January 1950 cited in   https://quoteinvestigator.com/2011/05/13/einstein-simple/   , [Accessed: 6 January, 2020].

Sharman C., (1997) 'Looking for Tomorrow's Leaders' *Management Today* August

Silverstein, A.J., (2010) *Islamic History: a very short introduction,* Oxford, OUP

Stacey, R. (1996) *Strategic Management and Organizational Dynamics.* 2nd edn, London, Pitman

Stacey, R.D., Griffin, D. & and Shaw, P. (2000) *Complexity and Management: Fad or radical challenge to systems thinking?* London, Routledge

Star, J., (2003), *The Coaching Manual,* London, Prentice Hall

Stodgill, R. M. (1948), "Personal factors associated with leadership, A survey of literature", *Journal of Personality,* 25 pp.35-71.

Stodgill, R. M. (1974) *Handbook of Leadership: A Survey of Theory and Research* New York, Free Press

Schedlitzki, D., Edwards,G.,(2014) *Studying Leadership: Traditional and Critical Approaches,* 1st edn. London Sage

Schein, E. H. (2010) 4th edn *Organizational Culture & Leadership,* San Francisco, Wiley

Schlechty, P. (2001). *Shaking up the Schoolhouse.* San Francisco, CA, Jossey-Bass

Shaw, C (2019) *Jurgen Klopp explains his approach to leadership* Available at: https://www.liverpoolfc.com/news/first-team/351529-jurgen-klopp-leadership-interview-liverpool   [Accessed: 31 Dec, 2019]

Shinagel, M. (2019) *'The Paradox of Leadership'* Available at: https://www.extension.harvard.edu/professional-development/blog/paradox-leadership [Accessed: 9 Dec, 2019]

Sinek, S., (2019) *'Leadership in Today's Society'* Available at: https://simonsinek.com/discover/putting-others-first/ [Accessed: 5 Dec, 2019].

Stefano, G., Gino. F., Pisano, G., Staats, B. (2014) *Learning by Thinking : How reflection aids performance* Working Paper 14-093 Harvard Business School

Sue-Chan, C., Latham, G.P. (2004), "The situational interview as a predictor of academic and team performance: a study of the mediating effects of cognitive ability and emotional intelligence", *International Journal of Selection and Assessment*, 12. pp.312-20.

Tabrizi, Sirous, (2018) *'A Comparison of Educational Leadership in Islamic and Western Countries and a Suggestion of a Model for a Global Society'.* Thesis (PhD). Electronic Theses and Dissertations. *Available at:* https://scholar.uwindsor.ca/etd/7400 [Accessed: 23 Nov, 2019]

Taylor, F.W. (2009) *The Principles of Scientific Management* New York, Cornell University Library

The Bible (2011), *New International Version*, London, Hodder and Stoughton

The Guardian (2019*) I'm not a villain: José Mourinho turns on charm before Old Trafford return,* Available at: https://www.theguardian.com/football/2019/dec/03/jose-mourinho-tottenham-manchester-united [Accessed: 6 Dec, 2019].

The Talent Foundation (2001) *Seven Factors for Business Success* London Talent Foundation

Toffler, A. (1984) *Future Shock* Friday Harbour, Michigan, Turtleback Books

Tuckman, B., Jensen, N, (1977) 'Stages of Small Group Development Revisited' *Group and Organisational Studies*, Vol 2 pp 419- 427

Turnbull, S., Case, P., Edwards, G., Schedlitzki, D., and Simpson, P. (2012) *Worldly Leadership: alternative wisdoms for a complex world ,* Basingstoke, palgrave macmillan

Tzu, S. (2009) *The Art of War* ,USA, Pax Librorum

Unis, I.J., (2014) *Moses on Leadership – a Qur'anic Narration* USA

Vaill P.B., (1982) 'The Purposing of High Performance Systems' *Organisational Dynamics* Autumn pp23-39

Weick, K., (2002) 'Puzzles in organisational learning: An exercise in disciplined imagination', *British Journal of Management*, Vol13, S7-S15

Western, S. (2008) Leadership: *A Critical Text, Thousand Oaks*, CA, Sage Publications

Whitmore (2002) *Coaching for Performance* (Third Edition) London, Nicholas Brealey

Whitmore J., Einzig H., (2003) *Organisational Synthesis: The Leading Edge* Performance Consultants, Unpublished

Whitley, R (1992), *Business Systems in East Asia: Firms, Markets and Societies*, London., Sage.

Woolfe, L (2002) *The Bible on Leadership*, NY, Amacom

Woodward C., (2004) *Winning!* London Hodder and Stoughton

Your Dictionary, (2019) Available at: https://examples.yourdictionary.com/metaphor-examples.html [Accessed 10 Dec,2019].

Yukl, G.A. (1998), *Leadership in Organizations*, New York, NY, Prentice-Hall.

Yukl, G.A. (2010) *Leadership in Organizations* 7th edn Englewood Cliffs NJ: Prentice- Hall International

Zohar, D. and Marshall, I. (2001) *Spiritual Intelligence* London, Bloomsbury

Bibliography

Aabed, A. (2006). *A study of Islamic leadership theory and practice in K-12 Islamic schools in Michigan*. Dissertation submitted to the faculty of Brigham Young University.

Adair, J. (1998), *The action-centred leader*. Reprinted 1993, London, The Industrial Society

Adair J., (2003a) Third edition *Not Bosses But Leaders: How to Lead the way to success* Guildford Talbot Adair Press

Al Suwaidi, M. (2008) *When An Arab Executive Says "Yes": Identifying Different Collectivistic Values That Influence The Arabian Decision-Making Process* Thesis (MSc) University of Pennsylvania

Ahmed, A. S. (2010). *Journey into America: the challenge of Islam*. Brookings Institution Press

Argyris, C. 1990, *Overcoming Organizational Defenses: Facilitating Organizational Learning*. Prentice Hall

Ashkanasy, N.M., Daus, C.S. (2005), "Rumors of the death of emotional intelligence in organizational behavior are vastly exaggerated", *Journal of Organizational Behavior*, Vol. 26 pp.441-52.

Avolio, B. Jung, D. (2000) "Opening the black box: an experimental investigation of the mediating effects of trust and value congruence on transformational and transactional leadership", *Journal of Organizational Behavior*, 21, pp.949-964

Bar-On, R. (2000), "Emotional and social intelligence", in Bar-On, R.,

Parker, J.D.A. (Eds), *The Handbook of Emotional Intelligence*, San Francisco, CA., , Jossey-Bass.

Belbin R.M., (1981) *Management Teams*, Heinemann

Belt, V. and Giles, L. (2009) *High performance Working ; a synthesis of key literature* Evidence report 4 , UKCES http://www.ukces.org.uk/our-work/research-and-policy/research-and-policy-analysis-series/evidence-reports/high-performance-working-a-synthesis-of-key-literature

Bennis, W. (1998) *On Becoming a Leader* London Random House

Berne E., (1964) *Games People Play* New York Grove Press

Binney, G. & Wilke, G. Williams, C., 2005, *Living leadership.* Pearson Education Ltd

Bluemel, J. & Mansour, R. (2020) *Once Upon A Time In Iraq -History of a Modern Tragedy,* London, BBC Books

Bion W., (1991) *Experiences in Groups and Other Places* London Routledge

Bolman L.G., Deal T.E., (1991) 'Leadership and Management Effectiveness: A Multi- frame, Multi-sector Analysis' *Human Resource Management ,30, 509-534*

Boyatzis, R. (1998), *Transforming Qualitative Information: Thematic Analysis and Code Development*, Thousand Oaks, CA, Sage Publications.

Boyatzis, R. (2001), "Unleashing the Power of Self-Directed Learning", in Sims. R. (ed.), *Changing the Way We Manage Change: The Consultants Speak,* New York, NY., Quorum Books.

CfE (2003) *Leaders and Managers: Learning Their Way* Leicester Centre for Enterprise

Charvet S.R., (1997) *Words That Change Minds: Mastering the Language of Influence* Dubuque Iowa Kendall/ Hunt Publishing

Cherniss, C., Extein, M., Goleman, D., Weissberg, R.P. (2006), "Emotional intelligence: what does the research really indicate?", *Educational Psychologist*, Vol. 41 No.4, pp.239-45.

Chowdhury, N. A. (2002). Leadership Strategies and Global Unity for the 21st Century: An Islamic Perspective. *Leadership & Unity in Islam*, 23.

Collins J.C, and Porras J.I., (1994) *Built to last: Successful Habits of Visionary Companies* New York Harper Collins

De Haan, E. & Burger Y., 2005, *Coaching with colleagues: An action guide for one to one learning* Palgrave Macmillan

Eraut, M. (2004a) *Transfer of knowledge between education and workplace settings* in: Rainbird H Fuller A Munro H (Eds) Workplace learning in context London, Routledge

Eraut, M. (2004b) *Practice based evidence* in: Thomas G Pring R (Eds) Evidence-based practice in education Maidenhead, Open University Press

Gagliardi, G., (2001) *Sun Tzu's Art of War plus its Amazing Secrets: The Keys to Strategy.* Seattle, WA., Clearbridge publishing.

George, J.M. (2000), "Emotions and leadership: the role of emotional intelligence", *Human Relations*, Vol. 53 pp.1027-41.

Goffee, R., Jones, G. (2001), "Followership: it's personal too", *Harvard Business Review*, pp.148.

Goleman D., Boyatzis R., Mckee A., (2003) *The New Leaders : Transforming the Art of Leadership into the Science of Results* London Time Warner

Gordon E.E., (2000) *Skill Wars: Winning the Battle for Productivity and Profit* Woburn, MA Butterworth-Heinemann

Gratton. L. (2014) *The Shift* London William Collins

Grint, K. 2005, *Leadership, limits and possibilities*, Palgrave

Grint, K, (2007) 'Learning to Lead: Can Aristotle Help us Find the Road to Wisdom?', *Leadership*, 2, 2, 231-46

Harris T.A., (1969) *I'm OK – You're OK : a practical guide to Transactional Analysis* New York Harper and Row

Harvey H.B., (1988) 'The Abilene Paradox: The Management of Agreement', *Organisational Dynamics* Summer : 17-34 taken from USGSB Managing reader 2002 Strathclyde University of Strathclyde Graduate Business School

Heron, J., 2006, *The complete facilitator's handbook.* Kogan Page

House, R.J., Baetz, M.L. (1979), "Leadership: some empirical generalizations and new research directions", *Research in Organizational Behavior*, 1 pp.341-423.

Huselid M.A., (1998) 'The impact of HRM practices on turnover, productivity and corporate financial performance' in Mabey C., Salaman G., Storey J., (eds) *Strategic Human Resource Management* London Sage

Jaworski, J. 1996 *Synchronicity - the inner path of leadership* Berret-Koehler San Francisco

Kahler T., Capers H., (1974) 'The Miniscript' *Transactional Analysis Journal*, 4, 26

Karpman S., (1968) Fairy Tales and Script Drama Analysis *Transactional Analysis Bulletin* 7, 26, pp 39-43

Johnson P., (2002) *Exploring Life in the Boardroom, Should we do it and how should we do it: a micro psychological perspective* Working Paper 2002 -09 (October 2002) Strathclyde University of Strathclyde Graduate Business School

Krausz R.R., (1986) 'Power and Leadership on organisations' *Transactional Analysis Journal*; 16, 2, 174-210

Laborde G.Z., (1998) *Influencing With Integrity* Carmarthen Crown House Publishing

Landy, F.J. (2005), "Some historical and scientific issues related to research on emotional intelligence", *Journal of Organizational Behavior*, 26. pp.411-24.

Lieberson, S., O'Connor, J.F. (1972), "Leadership and organizational performance: a study of large corporations", *American Sociological Review*, 37 pp.117-30.

Lindblom C.E., (1959) 'The Science of Muddling Through', *Public Administration Review,* 19:70-88, taken from USGSB Managing reader 2002 Strathclyde University of Strathclyde Graduate Business School

MacLeod, D. and Clarke, N. (2009) *Engaging for Success; enhancing performance through employee engagement*

http://www.berr.gov.uk/whatwedo/employment/employee-engagement/index.html

March J.G., (1994) *A Primer on Decision Making: How decisions Happen* Chapter 1, 1-35 - taken from USGSB Managing reader 2002 Strathclyde University of Strathclyde Graduate Business School

Mathews, G., Roberts, R.D., Zeidner, M. (2004), "Seven myths about emotional intelligence", *Psychological Inquiry,* 15. pp.179-96.

Mayer, J.D., Salovey, P. (1993), "The intelligence of emotional intelligence", *Intelligence,* 17. pp.433-42.

Northouse, P. G. (2012). *Leadership: Theory and practice.* New Delhi, India: Sage Publications.

Peters T.J., Waterman R.H., (1982) *In Search of Excellence* Harper & Row

Pugh D.S., Hickson D.J., (1989) 'The Management of Organisations', *Writers on Organisations,* 4th edn 84, 91-101 and 5th edn 95-129 - taken from USGSB Managing reader 2002

Richardson J., (1987) *The Magic of Rapport: How You Can Gain Personal Power in any Situation* Capitola CA, Meta Publications

Robbins A., (2001) *Unlimited Power: The new science of personal achievement* London Pocket Books

Roueche, J. E., Baker III, G. A., & Rose, R. R. (2014). *Shared vision: Transformational leadership in American community colleges.* Rowman & Littlefield.

Rush, M. (2002). *Management: The biblical approach.* Colorado Spring, CO: Cook Communication Ministers

Smith R., (1996) *Up Your Aspirations* Rugby Pau Publications

Thomson K.M., (2002) *The Company Culture Cookbook* London Prentice Hall

Waterhouse, L. (2006), "Multiple intelligences, the Mozart effect, and emotional intelligence: a critical review", *Educational Psychologist*, 41. 4, pp.207-25

Williams, J, (1998) *Don't they know it's Friday? : cross cultural considerations for business and life in the Gulf* London Motivate Publishing

Wirba, A. V. (2017). *Leadership from an Islamic and Western Perspective.* Chartridge Books Oxford.